A Bloody Legacy

Chronicles of American Murder

A Bloody Legacy

Chronicles of American Murder

**Mark Sabljak and
Martin H. Greenberg**

Gramercy Books
New York / Avenel, New Jersey

To J.P.
You showed us the courage to battle the odds.
And to the family and friends who supported him.

Copyright © 1992 by Mark Sabljak and Martin H. Greenberg.

First published in 1992 by Gramercy Books, distributed by Outlet Book
Company, Inc., a Random House Company, 40 Engelhard Avenue, Avenel,
New Jersey 07001

Printed and bound in the United States of America

Library of Congress Cataloging-in-Publication Data

Sabljak, Mark.
    A bloody legacy : chronicles of American murder / Mark Sabljak,
Martin H. Greenberg.
    p.   cm.
    ISBN 0-517-06006-X
    1. Murder—United States—History.   I. Greenberg, Martin Harry.
    HV6524.S23   1992
    364.1'523'0973—dc20   91-42047
                                                             CIP

            8   7   6   5   4   3   2   1

CONTENTS

....

INTRODUCTION

MURDER IS COMMITTED FOR LOVE. It is committed for hate. It may be motivated by a desire for money or for power. The underlying emotion may be jealousy or lust. And sometimes, murder is committed for no real reason at all—perhaps just for a thrill. Some murderers are poor, others are rich. Some are sane and others insane. Some are brilliant. Others are just plain stupid. A murderer may be male or female, old or young. In most cases, murderers are ordinary citizens unknown to the general public before they commit their crimes. But afterward, they become part of the snapshot history that is forever inscribed in the public memory.

This is a book about murders and the people who commit them. While it chronicles some of the most famous murders in American history, it also includes many offbeat, bizarre murders that never made national headlines. It is certainly not meant to memorialize murderers. Nor is it intended to be comprehensive.

Whenever possible, I have tried to ascertain why a particular murder was committed. In some cases, the reasons seem simple. Revenge was the reason Harry Thaw killed the famous architect Stanford White in 1906 and Walter Leroy Moody, Jr., mailed bombs to a federal judge and others in 1989. But in many cases presented in this book, the reasons will forever remain unknown.

There is no glory in murder; there is only heartbreak and misery. This book was not written in praise of murderers. Should we remember anyone, let it be the victims.

MARK SABLJAK

Date: Late 1777, early 1778

Site: Brookfield, Massachusetts

Type: Passion

Murderer: Bathsheba Spooner

Victim: Joshua Spooner

••

THE EXECUTION OF Bathsheba Spooner and her three co-conspirators in 1778 was significant for two reasons: It concluded the first capital case tried in American jurisdiction in Massachusetts, and the last in which a woman was sentenced to death in that state.

Bathsheba, the thirty-one-year-old daughter of a British official, had married sixty-three-year-old Joshua Spooner in 1776. The two were rumored to be Tory sympathizers, so when Bathsheba took in a wounded Revolutionary Army soldier, her husband actually considered it a stroke of good luck.

But he wasn't so lucky after all. Months later, when Bathsheba found herself pregnant by the young soldier, she decided that her elderly husband had to go. With the aid of two passing British soldiers, Bathsheba and her lover clubbed Spooner to death and dumped him in a well. A maid who went to the well the next day found blood in the water, and the body was discovered.

When the soldiers displayed wares belonging to Joshua, and servants told of overhearing the four plot the murder, they were taken into custody.

Bathsheba did not deny her guilt. But after her attorney failed to win her acquittal with a defense of insanity, she confided to a visiting clergyman that she was pregnant.

When the clergyman repeated her claim, which, if true, would probably have voided her sentence, she was subjected to an independent test by midwives and matrons. The group said she was not pregnant. A second group also checked Bathsheba, and though several of those examiners said she was indeed pregnant, the court upheld the death sentence.

Spooner was hanged on July 2, 1778, and—as she requested before her death—an autopsy was performed immediately afterward. A five- to six-month-old fetus was found in her womb.

Date: 1805

Site: Cooperstown, New York

Type: Insanity

Murderer: Stephen Arnold

Victim: 6-year-old Betsy Van Amburgh

....

STEPHEN ARNOLD came as close to the death penalty as one possibly can, only to have his life spared at the last possible moment.

Arnold was a schoolteacher in his thirties who lived in Cooperstown, New York. A true perfectionist, he showed no favoritism towards any of his students, not even his niece, Betsy Van Amburgh. When six-year-old Betsy misspelled a word, Arnold flew into a rage. He grabbed a club and beat the child to death.

Arnold then fled to Pittsburgh, where he tried to hide, under an assumed identity, but he was caught, tried, and sentenced to be hanged.

The whole town turned out for his execution. There were marching bands, a company of artillery, and a full battalion of infantry leading Arnold's way to the gallows.

As he stood there with a noose around his neck, Arnold listened to a minister give an hour-long sermon. Then he said a few words himself. Finally, the hangman closed in and the crowd tensed. But suddenly the sheriff stepped forward and took the noose from Arnold's neck. The governor had reprieved him.

It was said the sheriff had allowed the situation to advance so far because he disagreed with the governor's reprieve. He wanted Arnold to experience as much dread as possible. Besides, he didn't want to disappoint the huge crowd of spectators.

The governor's reprieve was based on his belief that Arnold had been temporarily insane. Arnold was later pardoned.

Date: 1841

Site: New York City

Type: Celebrity

Murderer: John Colt

Victim: Samuel Adams

THERE WERE MANY who said that John Colt, brother of Samuel Colt (who invented the revolver) and a member of a wealthy, prominent New York family, would never hang for the murder he committed.

They were right: The hot-tempered twenty-two-year-old Colt had hired Samuel Adams to print a book he had written. The two argued over the matter and Colt killed Adams.

Colt was found guilty and sentenced to hang, the typical punishment for his crime. But his stay in Manhattan's newly built prison, the Tombs, was hardly typical.

Colt's preferential treatment included food brought in from a hotel—including fowl and cognac. For prison garb he had silk robes and slippers. Most important, Colt was allowed to marry Caroline Henshaw on November 18, the very morning he was to be hanged.

Workmen finishing the gallows politely stopped hammering when the vows were exchanged so the crowd outside could hear every word. A silk curtain was placed across the cell door, and champagne was served.

Finally, however, the new Mrs. Colt was asked to leave so the execution could begin. But it was the minister sent to attend to the prisoner in his last minutes who rushed out of the cell to say Colt had stabbed himself to death—ostensibly with a knife smuggled in by his bride.

At the same time, fire broke out in the prison. In all the smoke and confusion, several prisoners were let out of their cells. One was later found dead.

Despite the fact that there was no official identification of the body, Colt was immediately pronounced dead, and burial took place at once.

But was John Colt really dead?

Years later, Edgar Allan Poe, who had befriended Colt before the crime, said he received a manuscript that he believed Colt had finished *after* the supposed suicide. Yet another friend claimed to have met Colt in 1852 in California, where he and his wife were allegedly living in splendor.

Date: Winter 1846-1847

Site: Wyoming

Type: Cannibalism

Murderer: Unknown

Victims: Unknown

THE STORY OF the Donner party is shrouded in mystery and shame.

The Donner party was a group of settlers heading West from Wyoming to California under the leadership of George Donner. Plagued by bad weather, they moved slowly and were eventually forced to stop at what was then called Truckee Lake (now Donner Lake) in the Sierra Nevada.

With heavy snows stranding them in makeshift shelters and food running out, a small group set out to seek help. The remaining settlers' supply of meat ran out, and when one of them died, some of the others ate his flesh. Before long, both groups found themselves either waiting for their companions to die or, in some cases, hastening their end in order to eat them.

The smaller party finally reached safety and sent rescuers back to retrieve the others. But of the nearly ninety people who had set off with the Donner party, only forty-five were still alive in April of 1847.

No one knows how many died naturally and how many were murdered. Only one trial was held afterward, and the accused man, Lewis Keseberg, was acquitted. He insisted that he had resorted to cannibalism only after his companions had died of natural causes.

Date: November 23, 1849

Site: Boston, Massachusetts

Type: Passion

Murderer: Dr. John White Webster

Victim: Dr. George Parkman

....

IT WAS CALLED America's classic murder, and it was said to have been the first such crime to gain national attention.

On November 23, 1849, Dr. George Parkman, a retired physician who had donated the land for the Massachusetts Medical School in Boston, visited Dr. John White Webster, a professor at the school, to demand repayment of a loan. When Webster insisted that he could not pay, Parkman, who had helped Webster get his position at the school, threatened to have him fired. Parkman had previously attempted to call in the loan by goading Webster—sitting in on lectures and making derogatory remarks about him.

After more threats, Webster later said, "I felt nothing but the sting of his words—I was excited by them to the highest degree of passion."

Webster was, in fact, so excited that he grabbed a heavy piece of wood and struck the taller Parkman squarely on the head. Parkman fell to the floor, bleeding from his mouth.

Unable to revive Parkman, Webster dragged the body to a nearby room and placed it in a large sink. Then he climbed in and cut Parkman's body into pieces with a crude kitchen knife. Webster put the head and smaller sections of Parkman's body into the furnace. Then he placed the larger portions in a vault used to store the medical school's cadavers, sealed the vault, and resumed his normal routine.

Parkman, of course, was soon missed. Had he been kidnapped? A $3,000 reward was offered for his return.

Meanwhile, Webster presented the school's janitor with a turkey, a suspiciously and uncharacteristically generous gesture on his part. Knowing about the reward and knowing that Webster's furnace had been hot on the day of Parkman's disappearance, the janitor put two and two together and pried open the vault. When he saw what was inside, he called the police.

Webster's trial drew national attention, with reporters gathering from all over the United States, and thousands of spectators lining up to watch. Webster pleaded not guilty, insisting that the body parts in the vault were those of an ordinary experimental cadaver.

But when a dentist identified the false teeth in the furnace as Parkman's. Webster was found guilty. He was hanged in 1850.

Date: April 14, 1865

Site: Washington, D.C.

Type: Assassination

Murderer: John Wilkes Booth

Victim: President Abraham Lincoln

···

ON SEVERAL ACCOUNTS, John Wilkes Booth's assassination of President Abraham Lincoln was not the success Booth had hoped it would be.

To begin with, Booth had been forced to resort to his second-choice plan. He had originally wanted to kidnap Lincoln and use him as ransom for Southern prisoners or possibly even a negotiated peace in the Civil War.

Moreover, Lincoln's death was meant to be only the first of four. Booth's other intended victims were Vice President Andrew Johnson, General Ulysses S. Grant, and Secretary of State William Seward.

And perhaps most important, the assassination was designed to elevate Booth, already very successful as an actor, to savior of the South. Instead, the murder of Lincoln on April 14, 1865, placed Booth firmly in the ranks of the despised.

After deciding that his kidnap plan for the President was too risky, Booth and six conspirators plotted the multiple murders, choosing the night of April 14th to act.

Booth began the evening by drinking heavily. Then he argued with co-conspirator George Atzerodt, who had decided he wanted out of the whole plan. Booth finally headed over to the Ford Theater in Washington, D.C., where Lincoln and his party were attending a performance of *Our American Cousins.*

There was as yet no Secret Service to protect the President, and his box was completely unguarded. Bored by the play, the guard who was supposed to be on duty had slipped away for a quick drink. But it wasn't quick enough. While he was gone, Booth snuck into Lincoln's box, and at about 10:15 P.M. he put a single bullet in the back of the President's head. The other male occupant of the box, Major Rathbone, immediately tackled the assassin.

After badly wounding Rathbone with a knife, Booth leaped atop the box's railing, yelled *'Sic semper tyrannis'* ("Ever thus to tyrants"), then jumped, breaking his leg when it got tangled up in a flag draping the box.

Lincoln's wound was untreatable, and he died at about 7:30 A.M. the next day.

Booth, meanwhile, had limped off to a waiting horse and galloped to the home of Dr. Samuel A. Mudd, who treated his broken leg. He then hid in the barn of a Confederate sympathizer, Richard Garrett, where Union troops tracked him down. When he refused to surrender, they set the barn on fire. As Booth stumbled toward its door, a shot rang out, killing him. Before he died he whispered, "Tell my mother I died for my country."

As for the other conspirators, Lewis Paine managed to stab the bedridden Secretary Seward, but did not kill him. He was arrested shortly thereafter. In the months that followed, he, Atzerodt, and two others, David Herold and Mary Surratt, were hanged for their parts in the conspiracy. Still others were imprisoned, including Dr. Mudd, though he was later pardoned.

Date: August 2, 1876

Site: Deadwood, Dakota Territory

Type: Assassination

Murderer: Jack McCall

Victim: Wild Bill Hickok

....

WILD BILL HICKOK, the legendary marksman, may or may not have been quite the hero he was made out to be. But there is no doubt that his death was less than heroic.

Hickok was playing poker in a saloon in Deadwood, in the Dakota Territory, on August 2, 1876, when Jack McCall came up behind him and put a bullet through his brain.

McCall, said to have been a drifter one step ahead of the law, faced a miners' court the day after the murder. McCall testified that he was simply avenging the death of his brother, whom he claimed Hickok had killed.

Apparently approving of this motive, and probably also as a reflection on Hickok's dubious reputation at the time, the jury found McCall not guilty.

Hickok, it seems, was well known as a shoot-'em-in-the-back sort of gunfighter. For example, his gunfight with the McCanles Gang in Nebraska, reported in 1861 as one of the greatest such battles of all time, was much less impressive than the stories it spawned.

The "gang," historians now think, was nothing more than three unarmed men and a twelve-year-old boy. And Hickok may only have killed one of the three men—while hiding behind a curtain.

Many of Hickok's exploits became more impressive with each telling. The duel in which he killed "savage" Dave Tutt, for instance, was actually nothing more than a fatal disagreement between two lifelong friends.

Even when he was hired as a U.S. marshal, Hickok was hardly a model citizen. For example, in Abilene, Kansas, he became known for extorting protection money from gamblers and pimps. And in a battle with a gambler, he accidentally shot and killed his own deputy (for which offense he was fired and forced out of town).

With his life rapidly sliding downhill, Hickok signed on with Buffalo Bill Cody's Wild West Show, but he found it degrading and soon moved on to Deadwood. He was shot dead there, holding a pair of aces and a pair of eights, cards known thereafter as a Dead Man's Hand.

9

Date: April 3, 1882
Site: St. Joseph, Missouri
Type: Assassination
Murderer: Robert Ford
Victim: Jesse James

....

JESSE JAMES was known as the greatest outlaw in all American history—a reputation that persists even today.

The James gang, led by Jesse and his brother, Frank, were great favorites of the ordinary law-abiding citizens who read of their exploits in the popular press.

Jesse was something of a Robin Hood figure. For example, after one of his hold-ups he was said to have stopped at the home of a widow. When she told him that she was about to lose her cabin to a bank foreclosure, Jesse reportedly gave her the $3,000 she needed to save her home. But no sooner had she paid the banker than Jesse robbed *him!*

True or not, this is the sort of story on which the James legend was built. But there were other stories that revealed another more cold-blooded side of the outlaw. For starters, Jesse led the first daylight bank robbery committed by an organized gang in American history. In Liberty,

AP/Wide World Photos

Jesse James

Missouri, the James gang robbed a bank of $60,000, shooting and killing a young boy who stood in their way as they headed out of town.

For years Jesse, who had been a Confederate soldier during the Civil War, along with Frank and the Younger brothers, terrorized banks throughout the Central states, making off with tens of thousands of dollars. While most of their well-planned robberies went off without a hitch, their luck ran out in what became known as the Great Northfield, Minnesota, raid. There, while attempting to rob a bank, the gang was set upon by townsfolk. Several gang members were killed in a gun battle and several more were captured.

However, Jesse and Frank escaped. They formed a new gang and continued robbing banks and trains. During one train robbery, Jesse killed a passenger and the engineer, which prompted the Missouri governor to offer a $10,000 reward for the capture of the James brothers—dead or alive.

Ten thousand dollars was a lot of money in those days—apparently too much for one member of the gang to resist. So, on the morning of April 3, 1882, after having breakfast and planning a future robbery with Jesse, Robert Ford shot James in the back. Then he ran from the house shouting "I killed Jesse James."

James's tombstone proclaimed that he was "murdered by a traitor and a coward whose name is not worthy to appear here." And Ford became known as the "dirty rotten coward who shot Mr. Howard." (Howard was the alias Jesse was using at the time.) The "murder," however, went unpunished.

After receiving the reward money and a pardon, Ford embarked upon a series of speaking engagements. But few in his audiences considered him a hero.

Ford himself later fell victim to murder in 1892, when an acquaintance of Jesse James blew him away with a double-barreled shotgun.

Date: 1892 to 1896

Site: Chicago and Philadelphia

Type: Mass

Murderer: H. H. Holmes

Victim: More than 20

··

IT'S IRONIC THAT one of the greatest mass murderers in American history was finally hanged for killing a man—after he had already done away with a reported two hundred women.

H. H. Holmes's demise came as a result of a dispute with his partner in crime, Benjamin Pitzel, that ended in Pitzel's death. His arrest for that murder led to the discovery of what came to be called Holmes's Murder Castle—a fiendish hotel he had built in Chicago. Some of the rooms were set up for torture; others were gas chambers; and still others had chutes that led to a basement crematorium, complete with corrosive acid and lime pits.

Over a period of four years, Holmes lured anywhere from twenty to two hundred women to the hotel by promising them jobs, or in some cases, marriage—on the condition that they brought their life savings with them. But before they could vow "till death do us part," Holmes killed them!

A former medical student, Holmes built the hotel in 1892 in anticipation of the Columbian Exposition celebrating the four hundredth anniversary of Columbus's arrival in the New World. But while many rooms were indeed intended for legitimate guests, a number of them were specially built for his victims.

The great mystery was how Holmes could have kept his diabolical crimes quiet for nearly four years. It was later explained that the women who applied for the jobs he advertised were told at their first interviews that they must maintain complete silence about the positions in order to foil Holmes's business competitors.

But Holmes was the one who finally was foiled after he and Pitzel designed an insurance scam that led to Holmes's arrest in St. Louis. While in jail, Holmes confided the plot to his cellmate, a man named Marion Hedgepeth. Holmes then offered to pay Hedgepeth to find him a lawyer, and Hedgepeth agreed. But when Holmes refused to pay up, Hedgepeth revealed everything he knew to the police.

Hedgepeth's story led authorities to Philadelphia, where Holmes had already murdered Pitzel, and eventually to Chicago, where they discovered the gruesome truth about Holmes's hotel.

He was hanged on May 7, 1896, in Philadelphia.

Date: August 4, 1892

Site: Fall River, Massachusetts

Type: Family

Murderer: Unknown

Victims: Andrew and Abby Borden

IN THE HISTORY of the United States, perhaps no other person judged innocent in a court of law was branded as guiltier by the world at large. Lizzie Borden, acquitted of the axe murders of her father and stepmother, never lived down the charges in the popular mind.

Although the real murderer was never found, there were many possible suspects. Andrew Borden, a prosperous bank owner in Fall River, Massachusetts, had apparently made many enemies during his climb to the top. Any one of them could have been responsible.

A mysterious stranger had been seen lingering around the Borden household on the day of the murders, August 4, 1892. Perhaps he did it.

The Borden housemaid, Bridget Sullivan, was apparently in the house when the murders were committed. Maybe she did it.

One thing is for sure, however, whoever murdered the couple must have been of strong stomach.

When thirty-two-year-old Lizzie stumbled upon the body of her father, he was lying on the sitting-room couch, apparently taking his afternoon nap. There were no signs of a struggle, but his face was a mess and the couch and the wall were splattered with blood.

Lizzie called to a neighbor, who came at once. So did a number of others. While the first neighbor comforted Lizzie, another began a search through the house, looking for Mrs. Borden. 'As I went upstairs,'' she later reported, "I turned my head to the left, and as I got up so that my eyes were on the level with the front hall, I could see across the front hall and across the floor of the spare room. At the far side of the other side of the room I saw something that looked like the form of a person.''

The person was Mrs. Borden, dead, grotesquely posed—on her knees on the floor, head down, rear end in the air—in a pool of blood.

A medical examiner later counted nineteen axe wounds on Mrs. Borden's head, and ten on Mr. Borden's. Taking a bit of poetic license, one newspaper account came up with the rhyme:

> Lizzie Borden took an axe,
> And gave her mother forty whacks;

And when she saw what she had done,
She gave her father forty-one.

In the days following the murders, Lizzie Borden came up with several conflicting alibis for the fateful time. At one point she said she was in the backyard; later she claimed to have been in the barn.

Authorities speculated that whoever committed the acts must have been splattered with blood. But despite several thorough searches of the house, no soiled clothing was ever found. Tongues began wagging again, however, when several days after one such search, someone said he saw Lizzie burning a dress. But Lizzie's sister, Emma, who was with friends on the day of the murders, said that the dress was covered with paint, not blood.

AP/Wide World Photos

Lizzie Borden

Another rumor had Lizzie attempting to purchase prussic acid, a deadly poison, from a local druggist. Could Lizzie have been trying to poison her parents?

Although the evidence against Lizzie was circumstantial at best, she was arrested, held nearly a year, and finally tried for the murders.

The prosecution played on her inconsistent responses to questions in the hours following the deaths. They also claimed that while Lizzie had originally admired her stepmother, the two had been at odds just before the crime because it appeared that Mr. Borden was going to disinherit both Lizzie and her sister. The burned dress was also played up.

For its part, the defense reminded the jurors of the magnitude and bloodiness of the crime, then pointed to Lizzie and said, "To find her guilty, you must believe she is a fiend. Gentlemen, does she look it?"

Apparently she didn't, for when the jury foreman pronounced Lizzie Borden "not guilty," applause broke out in the courtroom.

Lizzie and Emma Borden inherited nearly half a million dollars and moved into a mansion. The sisters later parted, and Lizzie kept to herself, doing charity work, giving money anonymously to a number of groups and individuals.

Lizzie Borden died in 1927, leaving small bequests to servants and the bulk of her estate to the Animal Rescue Leagues of Fall River and Washington, D.C. She left nothing to her sister.

Despite the verdict, many still believe Lizzie committed the murders. But as late as 1961, a group called the Friends of Lizzie Borden made up of such well-known mystery writers as Rex Stout, Erle Stanley Gardner, and Ellery Queen, dedicated itself to the exoneration of "Fall River's most famous woman."

Date: April 3, 1895, and an undetermined date
　　　 later that month

Site: San Francisco

Type: Sex

Murderer: William "Theo" Durrant

Victims: Blanche Lamont and Minnie Williams

THE STORY OF William "Theo" Durrant conjures up images of the Hunchback of Notre Dame, the Phantom of the Opera—or possibly even Dr. Jekyll and Mr. Hyde.

The murderer was a promising twenty-three-year-old medical student, a devout churchgoer and church librarian. Nevertheless, Theo Durrant took eighteen-year-old Blanche Lamont to his church library and proceeded to take off his own clothes. When she screamed, he killed her, dragged her up to the church's belfry, and sexually assaulted her dead body. He later calmly appeared at a church function.

When questioned about the girl's disappearance—he had been seen with her on previous occasions—Durrant spun a tale about white slavers kidnapping her. Slavers were indeed operating in that area at the time, so the explanation seemed to make sense.

Durrant might have remained free had he quit while he was ahead. But later that month he struck again. This time his victim was twenty-year-old Minnie Williams. Despite her willingness to have sex with him, Durrant viciously murdered Williams, also in the church library. This time, however, he hid the body in a closet.

The police later discovered Williams's purse in Durrant's suit—and Lamont's body still lying in the church belfry.

Durrant was hanged in 1898, his request for some final words denied. His parents, who had attended the execution, were presented with the body while they were eating a meal provided by the warden. Shortly thereafter Durrant's mother was heard to say, "Papa, I'd like some more of that roast."

Date: September 6, 1901

Site: Buffalo, New York

Type: Assassination

Murderer: Leon Czolgosz

Victim: President William McKinley

• •

HE WAS, AS ONE prison guard put it, "the last man in the crowd we would have picked out as dangerous." But Leon Czolgosz, a self-avowed anarchist, was deadly indeed.

On September 6, 1901, Czolgosz stepped out of a line of people waiting to shake hands with President William McKinley at the Pan-American Exposition in Buffalo, New York. He then pulled a pistol from under a phony bandage on his hand and fired point-blank into the President's stomach, crying, "I done my duty."

As he stumbled back into the arms of guards and aides, the President said, "Be easy with him, boys."

But fate did not go easy either on Czolgosz or on McKinley. The President succumbed to gangrene of the pancreas caused by the bullet—and what is believed to be poor medical care.

Czolgosz, twenty-eight at the time of the assassination, offered no defense at his trial, which was held less than two weeks after the murder. He simply said, "I killed the President because he was the enemy of the good people—the good working people. I am not sorry for my crime."

A little more than a month later, Czolgosz died in the electric chair in New York State's Auburn prison. Acid was then poured on the body, which experts predicted would decompose within twelve hours.

Date: June 25, 1906

Site: New York, New York

Type: Revenge

Murderer: Harry Thaw

Victim: Stanford White

....

THERE WAS LITTLE DOUBT that Harry Thaw put a gun to the head of world-famous architect Stanford White. Thaw fired three shots, killing him instantly, in front of a huge audience at Madison Square Garden.

And yet a jury refused to find Thaw guilty.

Thaw was a very well known and wealthy figure in New York society at the time. His defense was simple and obviously effective: According to Thaw, his beautiful wife had been defiled by White. As a result, Thaw claimed, he was temporarily seized by what he called dementia Americana—the condition in which a man believes his wife is sacred, and that if her honor is compromised he must take the law into his own hands.

Along with his reputation as one of the best architects in the United States, White had earned another reputation. He was known for enticing young women to have sex with him in his apartment.

One of the women had been Evelyn Nesbit, who became White's mistress at the age of sixteen. Nesbit was a beguiling teenager who soon began a career as a model and actress.

In 1905, at the age of nineteen, Nesbit married Thaw, who was the heir to a Pennsylvania fortune said to be worth nearly $40 million.

But the newlyweds did not live happily ever after because Thaw could not contain his jealousy of White. He was apparently unable to put the foul picture of White and the young unmarried Nesbit out of his mind—until the night of June 25, 1906, that is.

That night, as Thaw, his bride, and some friends were leaving a play on the roof of the Madison Square Garden, Thaw noticed White still seated in the audience. While Evelyn and her entourage went on ahead, Thaw lingered.

"I walked straight toward White," Thaw said later, "and about fifteen feet away, I took out my revolver. He knew me and he was rising and held his right hand toward, I think, his gun. And I wanted to let him try, but a man, a dozen men, might have maimed me, cut off the light, allowing him to escape and rape more American girls as he had too many —as he had ruined Evelyn.

"I shot him twelve feet away. I felt sure he was dead, but I wanted to

19

take no chances; I walked toward him and fired two more shots. He dropped. . . ."

Thaw did not try to run, and he was taken immediately to jail. His family mounted the best possible defense, and stories of White's womanizing and Thaw's valiant effort to save his wife's name were spread. The trial itself turned into a media circus, with tickets being scalped for hundreds of dollars each.

During the trial, Thaw cried out from time to time, a crazed gleam in his eye. But the jury was unable to agree on a verdict. Months later, however, a new trial was held, and this time Thaw was found not guilty by reason of insanity.

Thaw was sent to a mental institution, from which he later escaped. Although he was recaptured, his family was able to keep him from being institutionalized again.

Nesbit eventually turned on Thaw, claiming he had hidden behind her skirts during the two trials, and the ill-fated couple were divorced.

Date: 1911 to 1919

Site: New Orleans

Type: Mass

Murderer: Unknown

Victims: An unknown number

··

THERE ARE MANY famous unsolved murders in American history. In most, an arrest is never made. But this was not the case with the wave of axe killings that plagued New Orleans from 1911 to 1919.

Someone was using an axe to murder Italian grocers, their wives, and their families. The police had numerous suspects, and they arrested several. For a time there were always at least two possible axe murderers in jail. Eventually, though, all were released.

The first three murders—all of them grocers—were committed in 1911. Then there was a hiatus until 1918, when the axe murderer struck again.

Using a chisel to get through the back door, the killer crept into the home of Joseph Maggio, where he found the grocer and his wife in bed. The bloody mayhem that followed was discovered by Maggio's brothers, who were summarily arrested for the murders. But clues left at the scene of the crime reminded police of the 1911 murders, and the Maggio brothers were released.

A month later the killer tried again, this time only wounding Louis Besumer and his common-law wife, who later accused Besumer of being a German spy. Besumer was arrested, then freed when she recanted her story.

The axeman struck several more times, killing a two-year-old during one attack. More arrests were made. One led to a quick conviction, later overturned. But months later, the axe murderer was still at large; there was another killing on October 27, 1919.

The gruesome murders ended as abruptly as they had begun, and the crimes were never solved.

Date: April 15, 1920

Site: Braintree, Massachusetts

Type: Robbery

Murderers: Nicola Sacco and Bartolomeo Vanzetti

Victims: Frederick A. Permenter and Alessandro Berardelli

··

THE MURDER CONVICTION of two men in a small New England town set off more criticism worldwide than any other American murder trial. Fifty-seven years later, even Massachusetts Governor Michael Dukakis got involved.

To this day, the debate over the guilt or innocence of this pair of Italian immigrants still rages. Though both men were avowed anarchists, their trial wasn't much of an endorsement for 'law and order."

Nicola Sacco and Bartolomeo Vanzetti were arrested for the robbery and murder on April 15, 1920, of Frederick Permenter, paymaster of a shoe factory in Braintree, Massachusetts, and his guard, Alessandro Berardelli. A total of $15,776 was taken.

Much of the controversy surrounding the trial came from the physical evidence: Sacco's pistol and the bullets used in the murder. One of the "expert" witnesses for the prosecution proved unable to reassemble the gun when asked to do so. Another was later discredited.

Even more damaging were comments made by the presiding judge, Webster Thayer, who called the pair "dagos" and "sons of bitches." Judge Thayer was also heard telling a friend, "Did you see what I did to those anarchist bastards?"

The antiradical tenor of the times may have tainted the jury, and one juror reportedly said, "Damn them, they ought to hang anyway."

Sacco and Vanzetti were found guilty, but enough doubt was raised for the governor of Massachusetts to convene a special commission to investigate the case in 1927. The group called the judge's conduct "unusual" but found nothing that could mitigate the death sentence.

On August 23, 1927, Sacco and Vanzetti went to the electric chair in Charlestown State Prison in Massachusetts. Their execution set off protests all over the world. Forty people were hurt in a demonstration in London and numerous American consulates were picketed.

As he sat in the electric chair, Sacco said in Italian, "Long live anarchy!" And in English, he shouted, "Farewell my wife and child and all my friends!"

After Sacco was electrocuted, Vanzetti calmly walked to the death chamber and, addressing the witnesses in English, announced, "I wish to forgive some people for what they are doing to me."

Years later, continued study of the case by impartial law students led to a consensus that the evidence in the case was insufficient for conviction, the judge was guilty of gross prejudice, and that the 1927 commission that studied the case was in error.

In 1977, Governor Dukakis of Massachusetts signed a special proclamation clearing the names of Sacco and Vanzetti.

AP/Wide World Photos

Nicola Sacco (with a mustache) handcuffed to Bartolomeo Vanzetti (hatless)

Date: June 11, 1920

Site: New York

Type: Unknown

Murderer: Unknown

Victim: Joseph Elwell

....

WHEN THE HOUSEKEEPER came to tidy up, she did not recognize the man dying of a gunshot wound in the living room of Joseph Elwell's New York mansion. But as it turned out, the victim was Elwell himself.

Elwell, a leading authority on the game of bridge and a ladies' man with a long list of conquests, hardly looked the part of a Romeo as he lay dying, since he was without his usual wig and dentures.

Who had shot him?

The police had lists of suspects.

It could, of course, have been one of the seventy-odd women in his personal address book, many of whom had left nightwear in Elwell's home.

But the murder weapon, a heavy .45-caliber pistol, seemed an unlikely choice for a woman. And it was hard to believe Elwell would have let a woman in without first donning his wig and dentures.

In any case, the women with the best motives were all able to substantiate their whereabouts at the time of the murder—between 7 and 8 A.M.

The killer could have been a robber; but then why was there a large amount of money still in the house?

Or perhaps the killer was a disgruntled bridge player. Elwell had made millions writing about and playing the game. And he had probably also made enemies.

It was even possible that some post-World War I intrigue had finally caught up with him. Elwell had been a secret agent for the government during the war. But again, there was no real evidence to support that theory.

No arrests were ever made.

Date: June 21, 1920

Site: Chicago

Type: Double

Murderer: Carl Wanderer

Victims: Mrs. Wanderer and another, unknown, victim

···

BEN HECHT will always be remembered as a great newspaper reporter. But while his stories still stand as models of descriptive reporting, he also deserves a place in law enforcement history for the part he played in breaking one of the most famous murder cases in the annals of Chicago crime: the so-called Case of the Ragged Stranger.

At first glance, the story seemed simple enough. On June 21, 1920, Carl Wanderer, a young war veteran, and his wife attended a movie, *The Sea Wolf,* at the Pershing Theater in Chicago. On the way home, Wanderer told police they were followed by a ragged man, who brandished a gun when the couple arrived at their home.

Wanderer said he pulled out his own pistol, and in the gun battle that followed, both the robber and Mrs. Wanderer were killed.

According to Hecht's report in the Chicago *Daily News:* "Carl Wanderer, freshly shaved and his brown suit neatly pressed, stood looking over the back porch of his home at 4732 North Campbell Avenue. His wife, who was murdered last night by a holdup man in the doorway downstairs, lay in their bedroom.

Wanderer looked at his gold watch, and his hand was steady. He smiled blankly at the back porch in front of him, and with his eyes grown cold, repeated, "Well, I got him. I got him anyway."

Hecht interviewed several neighbors, none of whom had anything damaging to say about Wanderer. In fact, one said that Mrs. Wanderer had told her "only yesterday she was going to be a mother, and was so happy."

Still, Hecht was not satisfied. The reporter had taken an instant dislike to the widower, who seemed almost unconcerned about his wife's death. After Hecht shared his suspicions with the police, Wanderer was brought in for questioning. He soon broke down, admitting that he had killed not only the stranger, but his wife as well. Sure enough, both the stranger's gun and the gun Wanderer had used both belonged to him.

Wanderer then described how he had recruited a tramp on the street, telling him that his wife carried large sums of money and would be a pushover to rob.

Despite a spirited defense, Wanderer was found guilty and sentenced to death by hanging. Newspaper accounts of the execution mention that Wanderer was singing as the noose was placed over his head. As one paper reported, "From one of the crowd of reporters watching the execution came the comment that Wanderer deserved hanging for his voice alone."

Date: September 5, 1921
Site: San Francisco
Type: Sex
Murderer: Unknown
Victim: Virginia Rappe

....

SOMEONE CERTAINLY KILLED actress Virginia Rappe. But no one ever found out how or why. And even though the "who" part seemed obvious, there never was a conviction.

Roscoe "Fatty" Arbuckle, one of Hollywood's most famous early comedians, was the only suspect in the case.

Rappe's death resulted from an incident at a wild party being held in Arbuckle's hotel suite in San Francisco. That much is agreed upon. But many other details in the case have been clouded by bribes, disappearing witnesses, and changing stories.

Arbuckle, who was thirty-four at the time, reportedly took the twenty-five-year-old Rappe into a bedroom during the party. Twenty minutes later, guests heard her scream, "I'm dying! He's killing me! I'm dying."

Arbuckle was then said to have emerged laughing and wearing Rappe's hat, entreating the other guests to take her back to her own room. The actress was found bleeding on a pile of ripped clothing.

Rappe died three days later. One official report said that her bladder had ruptured when the three-hundred-pound actor forced himself upon her. Other reports said Arbuckle had stabbed her with a jagged piece of ice or glass from a broken champagne bottle.

Eventually, Arbuckle was charged. The first trial and then a second ended in hung juries. The third jury not only voted him not guilty but added: "Acquittal is not enough for Roscoe Arbuckle. We feel a great injustice has been done him, and there was not the slightest proof to connect him in any way with the commission of any crime."

Exoneration came too late, however. Details of his decadent lifestyle that emerged during the trial ruined his reputation and his film career. His former fans seemed particularly offended to learn that Arbuckle possessed a $25,000 Rolls Royce, complete with a toilet.

For the next twelve years, Fatty played some vaudeville and less-than-glamorous cabarets.

In 1933 he finally talked a studio into putting him back on screen. But the day after the project was completed, Arbuckle died of a heart attack.

Date: February 1, 1922
Site: Hollywood, California
Type: Celebrity
Murderer: Unknown
Victim: William Desmond Taylor

....

IT WAS CALLED Hollywood's most famous unsolved murder mystery. And it lived up to its setting, with several scenes that would have made a fascinating—if hard-to-believe—movie.

Taylor was the chief director for Famous Players-Lasky, a subsidiary studio of Paramount Pictures. A former silent-film actor, he was well known as a ladies' man, a fact that became even better known after his murder some time on the night of February 1, 1922.

When Taylor's butler opened the door the next morning, he found his employer lying on the floor with his arms at his side and dried blood around his mouth.

The butler ran into the street screaming, but instead of calling the police, the neighbors—themselves film people—began a chain of phone calls that brought a long line of other Hollywood figures into the house, all determined to clean up the residence, either to protect Taylor's reputation or their own.

One film executive, Charles Eyton, demanded that all alcohol bottles be removed from the residence.

Adolph Zukor, the boss at Paramount, ordered a search for anything that could damage the studio's reputation.

A fire was begun in the fireplace.

Actress Mabel Normand came in and immediately began an unsuccessful search for some personal letters she had sent to Taylor.

When the police and the coroner finally did arrive, the examination of the body began. Only then was it discovered that Taylor had been murdered—shot twice in the back with a .38-caliber handgun.

One neighbor said, "I wasn't sure then that it was a shot at all, but I distinctly heard an explosion. Then I glanced out of my window, and I saw a man leaving the house and going down the walk. I suppose it was a man. It was dressed like a man, but, you know, funny-looking. It was dressed in a heavy coat with a muffler around the chin and a cap pulled down over the eyes. But it walked like a woman—quick little steps and broad hips and short legs."

The list of suspects included Mary Miles Minter, a promising starlet, whose love letters to Taylor were quite suggestive; Minter's mother, Charlotte Shelby, who owned a .38-caliber revolver; and Taylor's former valet-butler, Edward F. Sands, who later turned out to be the murder victim's own brother (whose identity had been kept secret from Hollywood for years.) Sands disappeared after the murder; authorities thought he left the country.

More discoveries came after the murder: There were pornographic pictures of Taylor in poses with many of Hollywood's leading women. The love letters from Mabel Normand turned up. And there was a hint of dope addiction.

The mystery has never been solved. Taylor was dead, careers were ruined, and Hollywood, which was already reeling from the Fatty Arbuckle case, was dealt another vicious blow in the public's mind.

Date: September 14 or 15, 1922

Site: New Brunswick, New Jersey

Type: Unknown

Murderer: Unknown

Victims: The Reverend Edward Wheeler Hall and
Mrs. Eleanor Mills

....

THE MURDERS OF the Reverend Edward Wheeler Hall and his mistress, Mrs. Eleanor Mills, were covered by no fewer than five hundred reporters, who wrote more than 9 million words on the subject for their newspapers all over the United States. In the end, however, the Hall-Mills case would remain unsolved.

What made the case so notorious? Sex, money, revenge, lies, and more.

Hall was the forty-one-year-old married Episcopal minister of the Church of St. John the Evangelist of New Brunswick, New Jersey. Mills was a thirty-four-year-old member of the church choir. She also was married.

That the two were involved in a passionate affair was not in doubt. A number of letters written in both their hands attesting to their love in no uncertain terms were found at the murder scene, a lover's lane of sorts not far from where they both lived.

Hall had been shot once in the forehead, while Mrs. Mills had been shot three times in the head before her throat was cut. It was speculated that the murderer had interrupted an assignation, that he killed them and dressed them again, then carefully arranged them in an embrace and littered the area with the love letters.

The bodies were not discovered until two days later, when another young amorous couple stumbled upon them and called the police.

Both Mrs. Mills's husband, James, and the Reverend Hall's wife, Frances, were notified. James Mills, eleven years his wife's senior, was a janitor at St. John's. He said he knew his wife had spent time with the minister, but he'd thought their relationship was platonic. The last time he saw his wife, he said, was the night of September 14. He claims that when he asked her where she was going, she had said, "Why don't you follow me and find out?"

Mrs. Hall said that her husband had left early on the evening of September 14 to attend to business, and that she'd spent a sleepless night when he didn't return. It was not until she met Mr. Mills at church the next morning that she learned Eleanor Mills was also missing.

Police, however, found a witness to testify that he had seen Mrs. Hall leave the Halls' exclusive neighborhood in the middle of the night with her brother, Willie Stevens.

Stevens and Mrs. Hall explained that they had searched for the minister at the church, and then (despite the fact that Mrs. Hall had already claimed to know nothing of his affair) they went to the Millses' home. Seeing no lights on there, they had returned to Mrs. Hall's home. Her story was corroborated by a servant.

The most interesting testimony, however, came from a strange character named Mrs. Jane Gibson. Mrs. Gibson, popularly known as the Pig Woman because she raised hogs, said that she had been near the site of the murder on the evening of September 14 and had actually witnessed the crime.

The Pig Woman's somewhat confused report was discounted by a grand jury, and so no one was indicted in the crime.

Years passed. Then the New York Daily Mirror reported that Mrs. Hall had paid the servant who had verified her story of the night of the murder.

As a result of this information, the case was reopened. Mrs. Hall, Willie Stevens, and another brother, Henry Stevens, were charged with murder.

The trial itself was as strange as anything that had preceded it. The Pig woman, reportedly dying of cancer, was brought in to testify on a stretcher. All during her testimony, which included an account of men wrestling, shots being fired, Mrs. Hall bending over a body, the Pig Woman's elderly mother sat in the first row chanting, "She's a liar, she's a liar, she's a liar," a service allegedly paid for by the defense.

The Pig Woman's testimony was all but obliterated when defense attorneys cross-examined her. She became totally confused, failing to remember how many times she had been married, to whom, and when or if she had ever been divorced.

The jury found Hall and Mills not guilty. No one else was ever charged.

Date: February 6, 1923

Site: Osage County, Oklahoma

Type: Robbery

Murderer: William K. Hale

Victims: Anna Brown and Henry Roan Horse

AMONG THE FBI's most famous cases is that of William K. Hale, "the King of Osage Hills."

In the early 1920s, Osage County, Oklahoma, was a place of great riches and even greater evil. Fueling both was the discovery of oil, mainly on land belonging to the local Indian population. That made the Indians fabulously wealthy. Unfortunately, it also made them the target of many unscrupulous individuals.

One of those was a local resident, William K. Hale, who managed to build himself a small empire, including the ownership of a bank, by preying on the Indians. Lying and cheating, Hale seemed somehow beyond the grasp of the local lawmakers.

In the case that finally brought him down, however, Hale tangled with the FBI. After engineering the murders of Anna Brown and Henry Roan Horse, he had the home of Bill and Rita Smith blown to pieces while he was conveniently out of town. The murders and explosion were all part of an elaborate plot to enrich Hale's nephew, Ernest Burkhart.

The Bureau was called in because Henry Roan Horse was murdered on government land. But even the FBI did not find the investigation easy. Fear and bribery kept people from talking. It took an undercover operation, in which four agents infiltrated the town, to break the case.

The Bureau closed in on Burkhart, who ratted on his uncle. But that wasn't the end of it. Hale was rich enough to give the government a tremendous fight. Four trials and a trip to the U.S. Supreme Court were needed to bring a sentence of life imprisonment for the criminal.

In the process of solving the Henry Roan Horse and Anna Brown case, agents realized they had solved well over a dozen murders. And they earned the gratitude of the Osage Indians' Trial Council, who voiced their "sincere gratitude for the splendid work done in the matter of investigating and bringing to justice the parties charged with the murders of . . . members of the Osage Tribe."

Date: March 15, 1923

Site: New York, New York

Type: Possible Robbery

Murderer: Unknown

Victim: Dot King

....

BEAUTIFUL, BLOND DOT KING, whose real name was Dorothy Keenan, was the toast of New York City early in the 1920s.

Married at eighteen, but divorced quickly, King took a job as a hostess at one of the many speakeasies that flourished during Prohibition. It was in this atmosphere that she began her acquaintance with various "sugar daddies" who showered her with gifts.

Dot's name began to appear in the New York gossip columns, which referred to her as the Broadway Butterfly. But the butterfly's wings were clipped on March 15, 1923, when she was found dead in her bed, apparently a suicide. Near the body was an empty bottle of chloroform.

Upon further examination, however, it was discovered that Dot's arm was twisted behind her back as if she had been placed in a hammerlock. There were scratches on her nose, eyes, and cheeks, as well as burns around her mouth, all of which seemed to point to a struggle. The death was soon reclassified as a murder.

The most obvious suspect was J. Kearley Mitchell, who had reportedly spent some $30,000 on King in single year. More significantly, Mitchell was known to have spent the night of March 14 with her. But although he claimed he left Dot at 2:30 A.M., no one saw him depart. And it was his yellow silk pajamas that were found stuffed under the cushions of a couch at her house. Nevertheless, Mitchell, the son-in-law of a prominent Philadelphia millionaire, was cleared by the police, who then tried to shield him from newspaper reporters.

Another prime suspect was Alberto Santos Guimares, whom King lavished with gifts, but who apparently responded by beating her. Guimares had an alibi, however. He said that he had been squiring a wealthy socialite, Aurelia Dreyfus, that evening—a story the woman verified.

The explanation satisfied few, however, and after Mrs. Dreyfus, mysteriously fell to her death from a hotel suite window only a year later, papers indicating that she had lied to protect Guimares were found in her possession. But no further evidence turned up, and the police said they had no choice but to let Guimares go free.

The crime remains unsolved.

Date: May 21, 1924

Site: Chicago

Type: Thrill

Murderers: Richard Loeb and Nathan Leopold

Victim: Bobby Franks

··

RICH AND WELL-EDUCATED, Richard Loeb and Nathan Leopold seemed to have everything. They wanted one more thing, however: to commit the perfect crime.

Loeb, eighteen, and Leopold, nineteen, were schoolmates at the prestigious University of Chicago. Both of their fathers were reputed to be millionaires. After committing a few minor crimes together, the pair decided to plot a murder for no other reason than to see if they could get away with it.

The planning took seven months. Finally, on May 21, 1924, they picked up fourteen-year-old Bobby Franks, a distant cousin of Loeb's, in front of his school. Before reaching Bobby's home, they stuffed a gag in the youngster's mouth, and beat him about his head with a chisel till he was dead.

Leopold and Loeb then drove to a culvert along some railroad tracks, poured hydrochloric acid on their victim's face to complicate identification, and stuffed the body in a drainpipe. They then went to Leopold's home to play cards and drink, and from there they phoned the Franks to demand ransom for the missing boy.

The "perfect" crime, however, turned out to be nowhere near perfect. Leopold's eyeglasses were found near Bobby's body. And a ransom note was traced to Leopold's typewriter.

When arrested and questioned by the authorities, Leopold and Loeb cracked almost immediately, each blaming the other for the actual murder.

What could have been a simple rush to judgment, however, took a dramatic turn when America's most celebrated defense attorney, Clarence Darrow, agreed to represent them.

Darrow did not even attempt to prove the pair innocent. Instead, he spoke elegantly, passionately, and at length, to convince the court that the two must have been insane to commit such a crime. He spoke of their childhoods, claiming that their superior intelligence was more a curse than a blessing. Darrow then turned his attention to describing the punishment that awaited the pair if they were found guilty: death by hanging.

Here Darrow's rhetoric was so effective that even the accused, who had clowned and laughed throughout the trial, seemed devastated by the thought of their impending demise.

Although Leopold and Loeb were both found guilty, they were not in fact hanged. Each received life imprisonment for the murder, plus ninety-nine years for the kidnapping. For his role in sparing their lives, however, Darrow was regarded by many as the victor.

But it is unlikely the murderous pair did much celebrating. Loeb was killed in a homosexual brawl in prison in 1936. Leopold, whose cause was eventually taken up by poet Carl Sandburg, was released in 1958 and died in 1971.

AP/Wide World Photos

Richard Loeb (left) and Nathan Leopold

Date: December 15, 1927
Site: Los Angeles, California
Type: Kidnapping
Murderer: Edward Hickman
Victim: Marion Parker

....

BEFORE THE LINDBERGH BABY kidnapping made Bruno Richard Hauptmann (see page 46) one of the most reviled criminals in American history, curly-haired Edward Hickman had a place near the top of the list.

Hickman, a twenty-year-old who was considered by many to be quite bright, wanted to attend college. But he needed $1,500 to accomplish his dream. Rather than get a job, however, Hickman decided that a quicker route to the money would be kidnapping, so he began casing Los Angeles's most expensive neighborhoods in search of a likely victim.

He zeroed in on twins Marjorie and Marion Parker, the twelve-year-old daughters of prosperous businessman Perry Parker. On December 15, 1927, Marjorie was sick and unable to attend school, and Hickman saw his opportunity. He called for Marion at school, explaining that the family needed her at home. Unsuspecting, the young girl got into the kidnapper's car.

Hickman then had his young victim write the following note in her own handwriting:

> Dear Daddy and Mother:
> I wish I could come home. I think I'll die if I have to be like this much longer. Won't someone tell me why all this had to happen to me? Daddy, please do what the man tells you or he'll kill me if you don't.
> Your loving daughter,
> Marion Parker
> P.S. Please Daddy. I want to come home tonight.

Hickman also sent notes to Marion's father, taunting him and threatening to kill the girl if Parker went to the police. He also asked for $1,500. But when the first payoff was arranged, police surrounded the area and Hickman did not make contact.

At that point, Parker received another note from his daughter:

Dear Daddy and Mother:
    Daddy, please don't bring anyone with you today. I am sorry for what happened last night. We drove right by the house, and I cried all the time last night. If you don't meet us this morning, you'll never see me again.

Love to All,
Marion Parker

Shortly after she wrote the note, Hickman strangled Marion with a towel. He then cut off her legs at the hips and nearly severed her head.

Assuming his daughter was still alive, Parker decided he had a better chance of getting her back without the police. Another meeting was arranged, and this time he met Hickman alone on the outskirts of town. Hickman drove his car up to Parker's to give him a quick glance at the girl, who was wrapped in a blanket and appeared asleep or drugged. After Parker tossed the money into Hickman's car, the kidnapper drove a short distance away and then dropped the girl to the ground.

Parker then pulled up the blanket, and found his daughter's mutilated remains.

A $100,000 reward was offered for the kidnapper's capture, and his description was circulated throughout the United States. Hickman was located a few days later, in Seattle, and was returned to Los Angeles by train. Thousands of shocked onlookers crowded stations along the way to catch a glimpse of the killer, who waved like a celebrity.

Hickman, who twice tried to kill himself, bragged of the murder to cellmates, eventually admitting it to the authorities as well. He told a fellow prisoner that he hoped to convince the court that he was insane, but he failed. He was hanged on February 4, 1928, at San Quentin.

Date: February 14, 1929

Site: Chicago

Type: Massacre

Murderer: Unknown

Victims: 6 members of Bugsy Moran's gang and 1 onlooker

....

To THIS DAY, the St. Valentine's Day Massacre of 1929 remains officially an unsolved crime. But few doubt that the man behind the murders of six members of Bugsy Moran's gang and a bystander was thousands of miles away building an airtight alibi.

At the time of the Chicago murders, Al Capone was sitting in the county solicitor's office in Miami, Florida, discussing possible future projects in that area.

Capone and Moran, it was well known, had been at odds for many years. The setup was made when a Detroit gangster told Moran he had some alcohol he could sell at a bargain price. Moran suggested a 10:30 A.M. meeting on February 14, a meeting to which he himself came late. Lucky for him.

At the appointed time, a black Cadillac similar to the models used by undercover policemen of the day pulled up to the meeting spot. Three men in police uniforms and two others, who appeared to be undercover cops, jumped out.

The "policemen" disarmed Moran's group, which included Adam Heyer, John May, brothers Frank and Pete Gusenberg, Al Weinshank, and James Clark, plus Dr. Reinhardt H. Schwimmer, an optometrist and something of a gangster groupie, who had unknowingly picked an unlucky time to be around.

Forcing the seven men up against a brick wall, the "cops" leveled their tommy guns and sprayed them three times—in the stomach, chest, and head. One of the gunmen then walked along and shot each of the victims in the head. According to reports, Frank Gusenberg crawled twenty feet toward the door, with fourteen bullets in his body. But although he did not die until he was in the hospital, he told police nothing.

Moran quickly pointed the finger at Capone, but still the police were viewed with suspicion by many. In fact, the local Prohibition administrator was even quoted as saying he blamed the police for the crime. The next day, however, he insisted that he had been misquoted.

Only one person was ever linked to the crime by evidence. In April 1930, Fred Burke, a professional killer, stood trial for the murder of a policeman in Michigan. He was found guilty and sentenced to life in prison. Weapons associated with the St. Valentine's Day Massacre were found in his home, but he was never tried in Illinois, a state with the death penalty.

The site of the massacre was turned into a tourist attraction until it was torn down in 1967. A Canadian business saved the bricks.

AP/Wide World Photos

Six slain members of Bugsy Moran's gang

Date: March 9, 1929

Site: New York City

Type: Inconclusive

Murderer: Unknown

Victim: Isidor Fink

···

IT WAS A PLOT that sounded like something from an Alfred Hitchcock movie. As it turned out, the great mystery filmmaker actually considered the story, but he rejected it for lack of a suitable ending.

What interested Hitchcock and such newspaper reporters of the time as Ben Hecht, was the death of Isidor Fink, owner of a laundry on East 132nd Street in New York City.

A fearful man who was ever concerned about the possibility of robbery, thirty-three-year-old Fink was known to keep the windows and doors of his one-room laundry closed at all times. But despite Fink's precautions, what sounded like gunfire in the room brought police to the scene on March 9, 1929. The heavy door was bolted from the inside, and they had to break a window to gain access.

Inside, Fink lay dead on the floor, shot in the chest and left wrist. It seemed like an obvious suicide—there were no signs of forced entry and no one could have gotten out of the still-locked room. Yet no gun was anywhere to be found.

Perplexed detectives literally ripped the room apart, looking for loose boards or some sort of device that might have pulled the gun out of sight —anything.

Experts were dispatched to the scene to solve the mystery. In the end, however, no plausible explanation was ever advanced.

Date: Early 1930s

Site: Texas, Oklahoma, Missouri

Type: Robbery

Murderers: Bonnie Parker and Clyde Barrow

Victims: At least 13 people

JOHN DILLINGER, the bank robber, said Bonnie and Clyde were punks who gave "bank robbing a bad name."

Certainly they were a bizarre and brutal pair: Bonnie, born in 1911, and Clyde, born in 1909, met in January 1930, in Dallas, Texas, where Bonnie was living while her husband, Roy Thornton, was serving a ninety-nine-year term for murder. When she met Clyde, Bonnie decided to leave her husband for a "better" life. Considered by some to be a nymphomaniac, Bonnie seemed not to mind that Clyde was a homosexual.

The two began a four-year criminal spree in the Southwest, robbing banks and stores in three states (though their take never amounted to much—their largest haul was just over $3,000) and killing people willy-nilly as they went.

One hot day in 1933, for example, in Oklahoma City, Oklahoma, Bonnie, who was driving, approached a police officer to ask for directions. "How do I get to Sixth and Main?" she said.

The officer explained, and tipped his hat.

Bonnie responded by producing a shotgun and blowing his head off.

Clyde was no nicer to cops. When two of them asked him what he was doing lurking in the shadows at a barn dance in Atoka, Oklahoma, he shot them both dead. And together Bonnie and Clyde killed two more policemen, as they fought their way out of a trap set for them in Joplin, Missouri.

Among the civilians they killed were John Bucher, a jeweler, whose store they robbed of $10, and a butcher who wielded a cleaver in his own defense when they robbed his shop—Clyde shot him six times.

At last, in May 1934, they were set up for an ambush: They planned to meet a fellow outlaw, Henry Methvin, in Louisiana, near the Texas border, but in return for immunity from prosecution for his own crimes, Methvin alerted the police. Bonnie was eating a sandwich while Clyde was driving, in his stocking feet when they arrived for the rendezvous. Six lawmen opened fire, killing them on the spot. Twenty-five bullets were found in Clyde; twenty-three in Bonnie.

Date: Sometime in the 1930s

Site: Elmendorf, Texas

Type: Mass

Murderer: Joe Ball

Victims: 12 to 20 women

••

THEY CALLED IT the Sociable Inn, and for the guests it was just that. Beautiful waitresses and cold drinks made the Elmendorf, Texas, saloon a popular spot. There was even some entertainment of a sort, as owner Joe Ball kept five live alligators in a concrete pool in the back.

But for the young and beautiful waitresses that Ball recruited from all over Texas, the job apparently left much to be desired. Few of the girls stayed around long, and most of them left no forwarding address.

Their whereabouts finally came to light when the family of one of the waitresses petitioned police to help them find their daughter, who had suddenly stopped writing home. Their insistence that the girl would not voluntarily have left the inn without telling them, as Ball originally claimed she'd done, brought police back to question him once more.

"What really happened to Minnie Mae Gotthardt?" Ball was asked again and again by investigators visiting his saloon on September 24, 1938. At last, in response, Ball walked to the cash register, rang up a No Sale, pulled out a handgun, and shot himself in the head.

After Ball's death, police uncovered a number of body parts near the saloon, and the awful truth became apparent: Ball had been feeding his pet alligators pieces of the waitresses who had "disappeared" over the years.

The authorities also received a phone call from San Francisco. A man who had once worked on a ranch near the saloon thought he had seen Ball feeding human body parts to the alligators. He told the police that he had fled Texas when Ball threatened to feed *him* to his toothy pets.

No one knows just how many times Ball killed, but at least twelve Sociable waitresses were never again seen alive.

Date: December 18, 1931

Site: Albany, New York

Type: Revenge

Murderer: Unknown

Victim: Jack ("Legs") Diamond

EVEN THOUGH JACK DIAMOND already had a nickname, "Legs," he earned another one the hard way: He was shot so many times that he became known as the Clay Pigeon.

The seasoned New York gangster had made many enemies. He took bullets in the arm and leg while acting as a bodyguard for his boss, Little Augie. Diamond lost so much blood as a result that doctors expected him to die. He didn't.

Years later, Diamond was cornered in his mistress's suite and shot five times. But he escaped death that time too.

Then in 1931, Dutch Schulz came after him. Again he was riddled with bullets and again he lived to tell the tale. Like many others, Schulz couldn't help wondering, "Can't anybody shoot that guy so he won't bounce back up?"

Diamond himself claimed he was unkillable.

But on December 18, 1931, while Diamond was in a bedroom with his mistress, a gunman held him by the ears and shot him three times in the head. This time Diamond finally *was* dead.

Diamond's wife, called to his deathbed, had to be pried from the body. The only person to attend his funeral, she was murdered herself two years later.

Date: 1932

Site: Phoenix, Arizona

Type: Unknown

Murderer: Winnie Ruth Judd

Victims: Helwig Samuelson and Agnes Leroi

···

WINNIE RUTH JUDD was once judged insane. But she may well have been crafty rather than crazy.

The story began in Phoenix, Arizona, where Judd, a married woman of twenty-three years became friends with a twenty-seven-year-old nurse named Agnes Leroi. They worked at the same medical clinic, along with Agnes's roommate, Helwig Samuelson.

Winnie Ruth Judd (left)

One evening, after screams were heard from Leroi and Samuelson's apartment, Judd, asked one of Leroi's neighbors to help load baggage into her car. The neighbor, who was a baggage attendant for the Southern Pacific Railroad in Los Angeles, was not only strong, he was also observant. He noticed a red fluid leaking from the trunk.

When he mentioned this to Judd, she quickly drove off without the trunk—but not before the suspicious attendant got her license-plate number. He then opened the trunk and to his horror found the hacked-up bodies of Leroi and Samuelson.

Judd's car was traced to her, and she ended up turning herself in for the murders. Although Judd insisted she had shot the women in self-defense after Samuelson pulled a gun on her and shot her in the hand, she was tried, convicted, and sentenced to hang.

After her trial, there was a hearing to determine Judd's sanity. Both her mother and father testified that mental illness ran in the family, and Judd did her best to strengthen her case by laughing, clapping, yelling, and tearing at her clothes and hair throughout the hearing.

She clearly made her point. Her death sentence was changed to life imprisonment in a state mental hospital.

Judd escaped from the facility seven times. Once she made a dummy of herself to fool the guards. Another time, she stole a passkey. Her last escape came in 1962. It took eight years before she was caught; she was living with a couple in California.

At a new hearing, where she was represented by attorney Melvin Belli, she was judged sane and sent back to prison. Then in 1971, the Arizona Parole Board commuted her sentence and released her. She was then over sixty years old and no longer considered a threat to society. She moved back to California to live.

Date: March 1, 1932

Site: Southlands, New Jersey

Type: Kidnapping

Murderer: Bruno Hauptmann

Victim: Charles Lindbergh, Jr.

....

THE "MOST FAMOUS BABY IN THE WORLD" is what newspaper headlines called Charles Lindbergh, Jr. So it was hardly surprising that when the only son of the famed flier was kidnapped, newspapers throughout the country devoted much of their front pages to the crime.

But if the shock of the abduction was great, it was nothing in comparison to the grief that swept the nation two months later, when—after a series of contacts with the real kidnapper along with many frauds had raised false hopes time and again—the baby's body was found several miles from the Lindbergh estate.

Apparently, the kidnapper had killed the baby only a short time after the abduction by crushing his skull with a deadly blow.

The investigation of the kidnapping became a national affair. New Jersey State Police led the effort, and the Federal Bureau of Investigation, among others, aided the search. Even Al Capone, in jail for income tax violation, offered his services. But few doubted that Al just wanted out of prison.

The best leads in the case came from evidence found around the Lindbergh mansion, including a ladder the kidnapper used to climb into the nursery. There was also the note left at the scene, demanding $50,000 in ransom money.

To negotiate with the kidnapper, Lindbergh used Dr. J. F. Condon, a seventy-two-year-old retired school principal, who had offered to serve as a go-between. Condon and the self-proclaimed kidnapper met in a cemetery, earning the latter the nickname "Cemetery John." Condon came to believe that this was indeed the man who had taken the baby. The man spoke with a German accent, confirming traces of German usage in the ransom note, and he offered certain details about the baby that had not been reported by the press.

On April 2, 1932, Condon and Lindbergh himself went to the cemetery, where they exchanged $50,000—including $20,000 in gold certificates—with Cemetery John, who gave them a note saying the baby was on a boat moored at Martha's Vineyard in Massachusetts.

Lindbergh immediately flew to the spot, but there was no boat and no baby.

On May 12, 1932, a passerby spotted a tiny corpse four miles from the Lindbergh estate, and the baby's father and nurse were called upon to make the identification. It was positive.

For the next two years, there were no real leads. But then in 1934, a man drove into a gas station in the Bronx and handed a gold certificate to the attendant for gas. The alert attendant checked the numbers on the certificate and matched them to a list he kept on hand of those involved in the kidnapping.

He jotted down the license-plate number of the man's car and then called the police, who traced the car to Bruno Richard Hauptmann, a thirty-four-year-old German immigrant living in the Bronx.

Once Hauptmann was arrested, the evidence began to pile up against him. Ransom money was found on Hauptmann's property, and wood in his attic matched the wood of the ladder used in the crime.

Bruno Hauptmann was found guilty and sentenced to death by electro-cution. Despite support from the governor of New Jersey, who had doubts about Hauptmann's guilt, he was sent to the electric chair on April 2, 1936, maintaining his innocence to the very end.

His wife believed him. As late as 1991, Anna, Hauptmann's ninety-two-year-old widow, petitioned the governor of New Jersey to exonerate him.

AP/Wide World Photos

Bruno Richard Hauptmann

Date: August 15, 1935

Site: Los Angeles, California

Type: Insurance

Murderers: Robert James and Charles Hope

Victim: Mary James

....

IT MAY HAVE BEEN one of the most bizarre American murders of all time. But as things turned out, it wasn't very hard to solve.

Robert James decided to cash in on a double indemnity insurance policy on his wife by murdering her. He and accomplice Charles Hope had a plan: Mary James, pregnant at the time, was persuaded to have an abortion on her kitchen table.

Tied down, she was blindfolded—supposedly so she would not be able to identify the "doctor"—and given liquor to ease the pain of the surgery. Then in came Hope, carrying a box containing two rattlesnakes. Mary's legs were thrust into the box and she was bitten by the snakes.

James and Hope impatiently waited for her to die. It wasn't going fast enough to please them, as the alcohol apparently slowed the effect of the snakes venom, so James finally drowned Mary in the bathtub. Afterwards, he placed her body in such a way as to make it appear that she had fallen into a pond behind their home and drowned herself.

At first, authorities believed James's claim that Mary's death was accidental. But they grew suspicious after discovering that he had collected on another insurance policy from a previous wife who had also met with an "accidental" death.

Charles Hope was eventually persuaded to testify against James, who became the last person hanged in California before the state switched to the gas chamber as a means of execution.

Date: September 8, 1935
Site: Baton Rouge, Louisiana
Type: Assassination
Murderer: Carl Weiss
Victim: Huey Long

••

MANY ASSASSINATIONS END with the death of the assassin and the birth of a conspiracy theory. The death of Huey Long, the Kingfish of Louisiana politics, is no exception.

While Long was loved and admired by many in his home state (he was a U.S. Senator at the time of his death), he was greatly reviled by others. One modern account says that he "virtually suspended the democratic process and ruthlessly used his power of patronage to create what some saw as a semi-fascist system of state government."

On September 8, 1935, Long attended a special session of the Louisiana House of Representatives. Accompanied by five bodyguards, the forty-two-year-old Senator was walking down a corridor in the state capitol when Carl Weiss, a twenty-nine-year-old doctor, stepped from behind a pillar and shot him in the side.

Long's bodyguards shot Weiss twice, but when he continued to struggle they shot him another sixty-one times. Long died thirty hours later, but the story lived on.

Some people were suspicious about the assassination, since no clear motive for Weiss's crime was ever offered. According to one rumor, Weiss had only bloodied Long with a punch and it was Long's bodyguards shooting at Weiss who had accidentally hit the Senator as well. A similar account had Weiss and the bodyguards firing at each other, with the bodyguards shooting Long by mistake.

Date: December 16, 1935

Site: Pacific Palisades, Los Angeles, California

Type: Unknown

Murderer: Unknown

Victim: Thelma Todd

ALTHOUGH OFFICIALLY CALLED a suicide, the death of Thelma Todd, a famous actresses during the 1930s, is considered a murder by most crime historians. And the less-than-satisfying way in which the death was handled and the many unanswered questions surrounding it, place this case among Hollywood's great mysteries.

Todd, who was known as the "Ice Cream Blond," acted in over seventy motion pictures, most of them comedies, starring with Laurel and Hardy and the Marx Brothers among others.

The final scene in her life was anything but comical, however. On December 16, 1935, she was discovered dead in her automobile in her own garage. Because the motor was running, a coroner's jury ruled the death accidental, the result of carbon monoxide poisoning.

Yet the verdict did not explain the blood on the actress's face and in the automobile. Nor did it explain the fact that several people seemed convinced they had seen Todd in the days after her death.

There were also rumors that organized crime may have played a role. It appeared that Todd had resisted efforts to turn the second floor of her popular restaurant into a gambling casino. No less a figure than Lucky Luciano was suggested as an unnamed individual with an interest in the casino. Maybe he had her killed.

Also suspect, according to the tabloids if not the police, was Todd's lover, director Roland West, who reportedly wanted to break off his relationship with Todd. Although he was never charged with the murder, West never made another film. He died in obscurity in 1952.

Date: Sometime in 1936

Site: Brooklyn, New York

Type: Organized crime

Murderers: Louis Lepke Buchalter, Mendy Weiss, and Louis Capone

Victim: Joe Rosen

••

THE FALL OF ONE of organized crime's most powerful figures ever was tied to the 1936 murder of Joe Rosen, the owner of a Brooklyn candy store who had threatened to tell authorities all about his background in organized crime.

Louis Lepke Buchalter was not a good man to cross. First arrested in 1913, he joined a gang that included Lucky Luciano and Legs Diamond. By 1933, Buchalter had set up Murder Inc., a killer-for-hire scheme, in which his gunmen could be hired to kill anyone in the United States.

Even as the authorities were closing in on Buchalter, he was able to parlay his multimillion-dollar bank account into protection from most of the criminal justice system.

But when the Federal Bureau of Investigation took up the chase, Buchalter gave in to an appeal by columnist Walter Winchell to surrender. On August 24, 1939, he gave himself up to director J. Edgar Hoover personally.

Imprisoned for a narcotics violation, Buchalter ended up back in court, accused this time of murdering Joe Rosen, a former trucker he had forced out of business and who was apparently thinking of talking to the authorities.

Still powerful even in prison, Buchalter was able to fight the charge for four years. During that time, Abe Reles, an organized-crime figure turned informant, began implicating members of Murder Inc., including Buchalter. Despite heavy police guard, Reles was later found dead after a mysterious fall from a tall building.

When it became apparent to Buchalter that he would not be able to beat the rap, he indicated some willingness to help the authorities. But he changed his mind just before his execution, apparently worried that by singing he would be signing his family's death warrant.

Buchalter finally went to the electric chair on March 4, 1944, accompanied by the hitmen in the Rosen murder, Mendy Weiss and Louis Capone.

Date: 1940s

Site: Albany, New York, and Grand Rapids, Michigan

Type: Swindle

Murderers: Raymond Fernandez and Martha Beck

Victims: Janet Fay, Delphine Downing, and Downing's 20-month-old child

··

THEY WERE CALLED the lonely-hearts killers, for Raymond Fernandez and Martha Beck targeted vulnerable women whom they swindled and in some cases murdered.

Fernandez and Beck met while they were members of a club that was formed to help individuals find companionship. Their method of operation was simple: Fernandez would woo the women, while the 280-pound Beck played the role of his sister.

Once the women were hooked, the pair would swindle them.

Fernandez and Beck were suspects in more than a dozen murders before they were finally apprehended for two of them.

The first was the case of Janet Fay, a sixty-year-old widow from Albany, New York, who fell for Fernandez. After traveling to Long Island to meet him—her fiancé, she thought—Fay surrendered her money. Then she was beaten to death and buried in the cellar of a rented house.

The killers next moved on to Grand Rapids, Michigan. There, they made the acquaintance of another widow, Delphine Downing, forty-one. After robbing her and feeding her sleeping pills, Fernandez shot Downing to death. Days later, the pair drowned the woman's twenty-month-old child in a bathtub and attempted to bury both bodies in cement in the cellar. Then they went out to the movies.

Returning to the Downing home, Fernandez and Beck were met by the police, who had been summoned by suspicious neighbors. The cement was still wet, so the police easily found the bodies.

Among the couple's possessions, the police also found some of Mrs. Fay's belongings. Because New York had a death penalty sentence for murder, Fernandez and Beck were tried in New York and sentenced to die at Sing Sing.

Date: January 15, 1947

Site: Hollywood, California

Type: Sex

Murderer: Unknown

Victim: Elizabeth Short (the "Black Dahlia")

....

IT WAS THE STUFF of a lurid Hollywood murder mystery and right in Tinsel Town's own backyard.

And while the "Black Dahlia" murder may itself have provided enough material for several stories or even a movie, it was the number of confessions the case attracted that made it so unusual.

Elizabeth Short was one of many extremely attractive young women who longed for a film career and, many said, would do "anything" to accomplish her goal. Among her gimmicks was an all-black wardrobe—down to her underwear—that earned her the "Black Dahlia" nickname.

On January 15, 1945, Short's body was found in a dismal vacant lot in Los Angeles by a woman walking with her child in the early morning hours. The body was naked and cut in pieces, with half the torso on the sidewalk and the other half in the weeds.

When the police arrived, the gruesome details became clear. Short had been bisected at the waist by someone who apparently had surgical skills. Her face was battered, her breasts were mutilated, and cigarette burns all over her body as well as rope burns on her wrists and ankles—evidence that she had been tortured before being killed. The initials *B.D.* were carved on her thigh.

Her fingerprints identified the victim as Elizabeth Ann Short, originally from Hyde Park, Massachusetts, whose last known address was in Santa Barbara, California. Short's birthdate was July 29, 1924, making her twenty-two years old at the time of her death.

The Short case quickly became a coast-to-coast obsession. Early clues included tire tracks near the lot where Short was found. But police were more interested in a phone call placed to a newspaper editor in Los Angeles by an anonymous caller who said things that only the killer could have known. In fact, he confessed to the crime and said he wanted to turn himself in, but only after he had "a little more fun" with the police.

He also said he would send some "souvenirs" to the newspaperman. A short time later, postal inspectors handed police a message in which individual letters had been clipped from newspapers to spell out: "Here is Dahlia's belongings. Letter to follow."

In the envelope were Short's birth certificate and address book. More than sixty men were listed in the book, and the police set out to contact each one. In the meantime, the killer sent another missive: "I've changed my mind. You would not give me a square deal. Dahlia killing justified." Nothing further was heard from him.

The police later arrested a twenty-four-year-old married hardware salesman from Huntington Park, California. At first the suspect denied knowing Short, but eventually he admitted he'd spent an evening with her. He was one of the last to see her alive, dropping her off at a Los Angeles hotel on January 9.

And while the salesman denied committing the murder, and was eventually cleared, many others confessed:

- There was an army corporal who admitted that he roughed women up when he got drunk. He failed to answer key questions correctly, however, including those dealing with the state of the corpse when it was found.
- There was a waiter who called the police and screamed his confession over the phone.
- There was also a dark-haired woman, a former WAC, who said she had done it because the Black Dahlia had stolen her boyfriend.

The Los Angeles area was plagued by six murders of women in the next months. None of them, however, proved to be related to the Black Dahlia.

When the detective assigned to the case retired in 1971, he said that he was certain he had never met the killer "face to face" even though he'd interrogated dozens of suspects.

To this day, the crime remains unsolved.

AP/Wide World Photos

Elizabeth Short

Date: September 5, 1949

Site: Camden, New Jersey

Type: Spree

Murderer: Howard Unruh

Victims: 13 people

••

HOWARD UNRUH left his mother a note asking her to wake him at 8 A.M. on the morning of September 5, 1949. She did so. Unruh then dressed in a suit, white shirt, and bow tie, and attempted to kill her at 9:15. Then, at exactly 9:20, five minutes later, he began a shooting spree that left thirteen people dead in just twelve minutes.

Unruh, twenty-eight at the time, had just returned to his native Camden, New Jersey, after serving in the army. Apparently he felt his neighbors were laughing at him behind his back.

On the fateful day, he decided to stop the laughter. After shooting a shoe repairman to death in his shop, Unruh walked to the barber shop next door and killed a six-year-old youngster who was getting his hair cut. Then he killed the barber.

Unruh's next victim was an insurance man. After killing him, Unruh went to Maurice Cohen's drugstore, followed Cohen to his home and killed him, his wife, and his mother-in-law. Before it was over, Unruh had also gunned down motorists, pedestrians, even a three-year-old.

Unruh finally walked home. The police arrived soon after.

While Unruh and police traded gunfire, an enterprising newspaper reporter called the Unruh home and actually interviewed the killer:

"I'm a friend," said the reporter. "I want to know what they're doing to you."

"They haven't done anything to me yet. But I'm doing plenty to them."

"How many have you killed?"

"I don't know. I haven't counted. Looks like a pretty good score, though."

"Why are you killing people?"

"I don't know. I can't answer that yet; I'll have to talk to you later. I'm too busy right now," he said.

At that very moment, Unruh was busy fighting off the effects of the tear gas that allowed police officers to swarm into the house and arrest him.

Why did he do it? "They were picking on me," he later explained.

Unruh was found insane and committed to a mental institution.

Date: December 30, 1950

Site: Southwest

Type: Spree

Murderer: William Cook

Victims: Carl, Thelma, Ronald, Gary, and Pamela Mosser;
Robert Dewey

···

IF A CRIMINAL is in part a product of his upbringing, consider the background of William Cook:

Born in 1929, in Missouri, Cook lost his mother when he was very young. His father raised him and his brothers and sisters in an abandoned mine shaft for a while and then he took off.

Separated from his brothers and sisters, Cook was placed in a foster home. His foster mother twice gave Cook a bicycle for Christmas, and twice the bicycle was repossessed.

Eventually, Cook got into trouble and landed in prison for robbing a cab driver. Then in 1950 he went on a rampage that terrorized the whole Southwest.

First, on December 30, in Lubbock, Texas, by threatening a motorist with a gun, he forced his way into a car and made the driver get into the

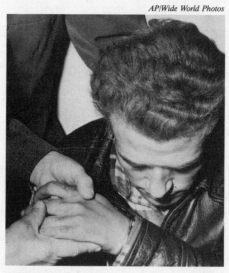

AP/Wide World Photos

William Cook

trunk. Cook then took off, driving until the car ran out of gas. (The driver eventually broke out of the trunk.) Cook's next victims were not so lucky. On the highway between Claremore and Tulsa, Oklahoma, he waved another car to a stop and forced his way inside. The car belonged to Thelma and Carl Mosser, who were traveling with their three children, seven-year-old Ronald, five-year-old Gary, and three-year-old Pamela. Even the family dog was in the car.

Cook held the Mossers at gunpoint as they drove from Tulsa, to Oklahoma City, to Wichita Falls, Texas, where Mosser attempted to shake Cook, at a stop for gas and food. But the criminal kept control, and they all drove off again.

They went to New Mexico, Texas, Arkansas, and back to Missouri. When a police car seemed to be paying too much attention, Cook stopped the car and shot all the Mossers, including the dog. Then he dumped their bodies into an old mine shaft.

Next he kidnapped a deputy sheriff whom he left unharmed. And after that he stopped another motorist, Robert Dewey. Dewey struggled until Cook killed him with a bullet to the head.

Cook kidnapped two other men, but then the word was out and he knew he was being chased. On January 15, 1951, he was arrested in Mexico. The Mexican police took him without a struggle and turned him over to the FBI.

Cook was tried and convicted of Dewey's murder in California and was executed in the gas chamber in December 1951, one year after beginning his deadly spree.

Willie Sutton

Date: March 9, 1952

Site: New York City

Type: Revenge

Murderer: Unknown

Victim: Arnold Schuster

IN FEBRUARY 1952, a twenty-four-year-old salesman named Arnold Schuster recognized Willie Sutton, a famous bank robber and one of the FBI's Most Wanted criminals, and called the authorities. Schuster became a national hero. But he didn't get much of a chance to enjoy his sudden celebrity.

After Sutton was captured, Schuster gave interviews to newspapers, radio, and television, who used his name, with his permission, although the FBI routinely advises people who turn in fugitives to remain anonymous.

So it was not so surprising that on March 9, 1952, Schuster was found dead on the Brooklyn street where he lived, shot twice in the groin and once in each eye.

No one was ever tried for the murder, but according to the unofficial story the assassination was ordered by a Mafia boss named Albert Anastasia, who exploded when he saw Schuster being interviewed, yelling, "I can't stand squealers."

Anastasia is said to have sent Frederick Tenuto, an escaped convict, to kill Schuster. But Tenuto, himself on the FBI's Most Wanted list, was never found. Rumor had it that he was killed too, to remove any link between Anastasia and the Schuster murder.

Anastasia, however, may have paid the ultimate price for the murder. Supposedly, the hit on this ordinary citizen so angered his fellow Mafia chieftains, that they had him executed in a barber shop on October 25, 1957 (see page 66).

Date: March 9, 1953
Site: Burbank, California
Type: Robbery
Murderer: Barbara Graham
Victim: Mabel Monahan

....

THE 1958 MOVIE *I Want to Live* cast a glamorous actress, Susan Hayward, in the role of a call girl who gets involved in several murders and winds up dying in the gas chamber. Hayward won an Oscar for her touching performance, which had added poignancy because the plot was based on the true story of a woman named Barbara Graham.

Graham was born in 1923. Her life was a pathetic tale of bad luck, bad breaks, and bad relationships. A runaway from a poverty-stricken home, she went from institution to institution and finally to reform school. She married several times, was divorced twice, and gave birth to three children. She was also arrested numerous times for minor crimes including lewd conduct.

Her last marriage was to a salesman, Henry Graham, who fathered her third child and introduced her to drugs. She then joined forces with four male criminals in Los Angeles. That group was tied to a string of robberies and the murder of at least six people, including several children.

Graham was eventually tried for the murder of Mabel Monahan, a crippled sixty-three-year-old Burbank resident. One of Graham's group, who later cooperated with authorities, testified that she hit the elderly woman in the head with the butt of a pistol to get into the house. When another group member screamed, "Give her more!" Graham allegedly responded by cracking the woman's skull with repeated blows. The robbery was unsuccessful, however, and the five were arrested.

With her cohort testifying against her, and her alibis discredited, Graham was clearly in serious trouble. But the final blow came when police planted an undercover officer in the prison where Graham was being held. The officer told Graham that he was an underworld figure who could provide an alibi for a fee of $25,000. Graham went for the deal.

When it was made public in court, Graham said, "Oh, have you ever been desperate?"

She appealed her conviction, but with two other members of her group also sentenced to die, there was no hope. At her execution she asked for a blindfold saying, "I don't want to have to look at people." She died in the gas chamber at the age of at thirty-three.

Date: September 29, 1953
Site: Kansas City, Missouri
Type: Kidnapping
Murderers: Carl Austin Hall and Bonnie Brown Heady
Victim: Bobby Greenlease, Jr.

••

IN THE LATE MORNING of September 28, 1953, a woman entered an exclusive private school and walked out minutes later with one of the students, six-year-old Bobby Greenlease, Jr.

The woman claimed to be Bobby's mother's sister. Bobby's mother had suffered a heart attack, she said, and wanted her son brought to the hospital right away.

The unsuspecting nuns who ran the school allowed Bobby to leave with his "aunt" in a waiting car. They then called Bobby's home to inquire about Mrs. Greenlease's condition. It was not until Mrs. Greenlease herself answered the phone, that they realized the boy had been kidnapped.

For nearly a week the Greenleases and the kidnappers traded phone calls and messages. But the parents were wasting their time.

Almost immediately after the woman, forty-one-year-old Bonnie Brown Heady, led him to the car, Bobby was murdered by her lover, Carl Austin Hall.

Hall, thirty-four, the alcoholic son of a respected lawyer, drove to a deserted spot, where he attempted to strangle Bobby, who fought him off. Hall then shot the child twice, once in the chest and once in the head, and stuffed the body into a plastic bag.

Heady, also an alcoholic, left the car during the murder, but as soon as Bobby was dead, she and Hall drove the body to her home in St. Joseph, Missouri. They had already dug a trench to bury him in.

Not until they buried him did Hall and Heady send their first (illiterate) ransom note, demanding $600,000 in small bills. "If do exactly as we say," they wrote, "an try no tricks, your boy will be back safe within 24 hrs—after we check money.

"Deliver money in army duefel bag. Be ready to deliver at once on contact."

The Greenleases received several phone calls from the kidnappers, whose identities were still unknown. With the FBI on alert, they agreed to pay the ransom, but instructions for delivery of the money were so confusing that the plans were never completed.

In one conversation, Mrs. Greenlease asked to talk to her son on the phone. The pair refused, saying that they couldn't risk bringing him to the phone.

The mother pressed them to ask Bobby two questions to which only he could know the answers. Later the kidnappers called again to say, "we didn't get anything from him. . . . He wouldn't talk."

On October 4, the ransom was paid. Hall and Heady then called the Greenlease home to say that while they hadn't counted the money, they were sure it was all there and would deliver Bobby within twenty-four hours. The Greenleases heard nothing further.

Meanwhile, Hall and Heady went to an apartment in St. Louis where Heady passed out drunk. Hall slipped away, leaving her with only $2,000 of the loot. But he bragged to a cabdriver, who called the police.

When he was arrested, Hall had only $295,140 of the $600,000 and Bobby's body already had been found and identified.

Heady, who blamed Hall for the murder, pleaded guilty in federal court. The two kidnappers were convicted and sentenced to death. They died within twenty seconds of each other on December 18, 1953, in the gas chamber at the Jefferson City State Penitentiary.

AP/Wide World Photos

Bobby Greenlease, Jr., with his father

Date: July 3, 1954
Site: Cleveland, Ohio
Type: Unknown
Murderer: Unknown
Victim: Marilyn Sheppard

···

THOUGH IT'S NOW listed as an unsolved crime, there was actually once a conviction in the murder of Marilyn Sheppard. The victim, thirty-one years old and four months pregnant at the time, was killed by more than two dozen blows to the head.

Her husband was home with her at the time of the murder. A prominent Cleveland doctor, he said he awoke to his wife's screams, but was knocked unconscious when he tried to fight off the bushy-haired stranger who was attacking her.

Dr. Samuel Sheppard and his second wife, Ariane

Dr. Sheppard, who was pushed to his wife's funeral in a wheelchair, wearing a neck brace, was nevertheless charged with the murder. The motive seemed clear: Sheppard was having an affair with a young female employee of the hospital where he worked. Testimony from both the doctor and his lover were crucial to the prosecution's case.

The verdict: guilty.

The doctor was sentenced to life in prison, but some people believed he was innocent. They organized a campaign on his behalf, enlisting the aid of several celebrities. They also hired famed attorney F. Lee Bailey, who helped Sheppard win release from the penitentiary in 1964.

Bailey then defended Sheppard in a new trial, which was held in 1966. This time Bailey called the case against his client "ten pounds of hogwash in a five-pound bag," and did not call upon Sheppard to testify. This time the verdict was not guilty. Sheppard went free.

Sheppard then married a woman with whom he had corresponded during his imprisonment, but she divorced him in 1968. He died in 1970.

The murder case of Marilyn Sheppard is still officially open.

Date: August 1955

Site: Chicago

Type: Robbery

Murderer: Richard Carpenter

Victim: A police detective

··

THE DESPERATE HOURS, a movie about three escaped convicts who terrorize a suburban Indiana family in their home, had an all-star cast that included Frederic March, Arthur Kennedy, and Humphrey Bogart. The story was based on the actions of Richard Carpenter of Chicago.

After killing a police detective and wounding another policeman, Carpenter made his way to the home of a truck driver, his wife, and their two young children and took the family hostage. Though he sat for a night and day in the living room, the adults did not reveal to the children that the visiting "friend" was holding a gun on them.

Carpenter had come from a broken home. He was a "mama's boy" who had turned to crime. In Chicago he had robbed more than seventy grocery stores, laundromats, and saloons. He would sit at a bar until closing time, then calmly pull a gun while he explained to those remaining that they could give him their money or they could get shot. He never had to use the gun.

But Carpenter's luck ran out when a police detective recognized him on a subway. As the policeman pulled out a wanted poster to assure himself of Carpenter's identity, Carpenter pulled out a gun and killed the officer.

Carpenter was next spotted sleeping in a movie theater by an off-duty policeman, who walked him into the lobby at gunpoint. There, Carpenter pretended to stumble, then pulled his own gun and fired. He hit the policeman in the chest but did not kill him. The cop returned fire, getting Carpenter in the leg.

Once again Carpenter escaped, and that's when he wound up at the trucker's house. In the living room he occupied, the hostages spoke calmly with Carpenter. Slowly they gained his trust. When he finally allowed them to go outside to "get some air," they escaped to a neighbor's house and the police were called.

The area was quickly surrounded. Carpenter ran to the roof, then crossed to another building, where he took refuge until the police closed in.

Richard Carpenter died in the electric chair in 1956.

Date: November 1, 1955

Site: In the air near Denver, Colorado

Type: Insurance

Murderer: Jack Graham

Victims: 44 people

WHILE SOME CRIMES offer little to lead police to the guilty, the bombing of Flight 629, a United Air Lines DC-6B just minutes from Stapleton Airport in Denver, was cluttered with clues.

Agents from the Federal Bureau of Investigation, called in less than a week after the plane exploded, were immediately struck by the fact that almost all the luggage put aboard the flight had been recovered; about the only thing missing was one of several items belonging to Mrs. Daisie King, a wealthy fifty-four-year-old.

In fact, King's recovered handbag contained a newspaper clipping which revealed that her son, Jack Graham, was being hunted by police for forgery. Further digging into the son's life turned up several arrests. There were two reports of insurance fraud: Graham had deliberately stalled a pickup truck in front of a train and had been responsible for a gas explosion in a restaurant.

On November 10, agents began questioning Graham about his mother's luggage and were told that Mrs. King liked to pack her own bags. According to Graham, she had done so before this trip. The next day, however, Graham's wife mentioned that her husband had given Mrs. King a large gift-wrapped package before she left for the airport. Mrs. Graham was under the impression that the "gift" was a set of tools.

The FBI questioned Graham again three days later, and this time they came right out and asked if he had bombed the plane. Graham not only denied involvement, he even invited the FBI to search his home. When they did so, the agents found a package of shotgun shells and some wire of the type used to detonate dynamite.

Graham later insisted that he had given his mother a gift of tools.

Even more damning—and harder to explain—were the $37,500 worth of life insurance policies on Mrs. King naming her son as beneficiary.

Finally, Graham confessed. He said he needed the life insurance money and the money that his mother had left him in her will.

Although he repudiated his confession, jurors convicted him in seventy minutes. He was sent to the gas chamber in 1957.

Date: October 25, 1957

Site: New York City

Type: Assassination

Murderer: Unknown

Victim: Albert Anastasia

··

LAW ENFORCEMENT AUTHORITIES generally do their best to solve murders, but here's one case where they may have made an exception.

The occasion was the assassination of an organized crime figure named Albert Anastasia. Known as the Lord High Executioner, Anastasia had set up one of the most effective divisions of Murder Inc., the killer-for-hire arm of the mob. He was personally responsible for at least sixty murders during his career in the Mafia—most of them accomplished with an ice pick or a scarf.

On October 25, 1957, Anastasia arrived at the barbershop in the basement of the Park Sheraton Hotel in New York City. His bodyguard, conveniently, was absent when he settled into the barber chair and allowed the barber to wrap a hot towel around his face.

Suddenly, two men burst into the shop, pulled out their guns, and headed toward Anastasia, yelling "Keep your mouth shut if you don't want your head blown off" to the barber.

AP/Wide World Photos

Albert Anastasia

Reports on the next sequence of events differ. Some say the gunmen fired while Anastasia still had the towel over his face. Others say Anastasia removed the towel and tried to run. In any case, the burly gangster was hit by at least five bullets, including one to the back of his head.

As the murderer-become-murder-victim fell to the floor, the gunmen dropped their weapons and left. Of course, there were no fingerprints on the guns. And no one stepped forward to identify the killers.

The list of possible suspects was long indeed. During his crime career, which began in the 1920s, Anastasia ruthlessly disposed of anyone who stood in his way. Despite numerous arrests for murder, and even one conviction, Anastasia had spent little time in jail. And he always returned to the streets to kill again.

Anastasia is credited with coining the terms *contract* for a murder assignment and *hit* for the murder itself. He is also said to have been the first person to use out-of-town criminals to perform murders.

He hired a stable of killers for Murder Inc. And when the occasional criminal was persuaded by law enforcement officials to "sing," Anastasia could somehow always count on a mysterious accident to eliminate the would-be informant.

In the end, however, Anastasia ran afoul of several of his fellow Mafia chiefs. In the days before his death, he was said to be planning a move to Cuba, to enter into gambling, in defiance of Meyer Lansky, who had already set up operations there. And Lansky was just one of several who wanted Anastasia dead.

Ironically, it was probably out-of-town hitmen who carried out the assassination in the barbershop, tearing a page from the Lord High Executioner's own book.

Date: November 16, 1957

Site: Plainfield, Wisconsin

Type: Serial

Murderer: Ed Gein

Victims: Mary Hogan and Bernice Worden

ONE OF AMERICA's most bizarre murder cases couldn't have happened to a more average American town. It became the inspiration for several novels and Alfred Hitchcock's film, *Psycho.*

When Bernice Worden of Plainfield, Wisconsin, failed to open her hardware store on November 16, 1957, a worried neighbor called her son. He entered the store looking for his mother and instead found a pool of fresh blood on the floor and a sales slip for antifreeze made out to Ed Gein.

The sheriff paid an immediate visit to Gein, who lived alone on a nearby farm, and there he found Mrs. Worden's body. It was hanging by the heels in Gein's shed, dressed out like a deer, with the head removed. But that was the least of it.

Inside the filthy Gein house, the sheriff discovered a "death mask" made from a skinned head, lamp shades covered with tanned human skin, a chair partly fashioned from human skin, and the upper portion of

Ed Gein

a woman's body mounted on a board. There was a human heart in a coffee can in the kitchen, and numerous bones—also human—were buried in the backyard.

Gein did not deny Mrs. Worden's murder, but he said he'd gotten most of the body parts by robbing graves. He then told the police that after his own mother's death in 1945, he had become disconsolate. It was during one of his regular visits to her grave that he'd begun digging up fresh graves of women who had died in middle-age like his mother.

Gein claimed that he could always feel his grave-digging spells coming on. Sometimes he would pray and the prayers would stop the spell. But sometimes prayer did not work. He robbed graves from 1949 through 1954.

Gein had actually killed two women: Mary Hogan and Bernice Worden. Both were plump and middle aged—just like the murderer's mom.

Gein was arrested and immediately sent to a mental institution. Then, in 1968, he was declared fit to stand trial and was convicted of killing Mrs. Worden. But the court ruled that he was insane at the time of the murder and sent him back to the mental hospital for an indefinite period.

Gein was petitioned for release in 1974, but a judge refused, convinced that he was still mentally ill. He died in 1984 at the age of seventy-seven.

The presiding judge, who wrote a book on the case, said that people were still calling him in the mid-1980s, for directions to the Gein farm.

Date: December 1957 to February 1958

Site: Nebraska; Wyoming

Type: Spree

Murderer: Charles Starkweather

Victims: 11 people

....

CHARLES STARKWEATHER was much shorter than James Dean, and his hair was red not blond. Nevertheless, Starkweather, who was nineteen years old in 1959, identified with the actor and considered himself a young rebel without a cause, a tough guy you wouldn't want to mess with.

Starkweather was passionate about three things: comic books, hot rods, and hunting. And because he had a hard time finding girlfriends his own age, he hooked up with fourteen-year-old Caril Ann Fugate.

On December 1, 1957, Starkweather drove into a gas station in his hometown of Lincoln, Nebraska, and robbed the twenty-one-year-old attendant at gunpoint. He then drove the victim to the open plains and killed him with several shots to the head.

Two months later, while the police were still baffled over the gas station murder, Starkweather began killing in earnest. Waiting for his girlfriend at her home one day, he got into an argument with Caril Ann's mother, who was nervous having Starkweather in the house since he had a rifle with him. When Marion Bartlett, Caril Ann's stepfather, also objected to the gun, Starkweather used it to shoot them both.

Caril Ann arrived home about then, but that didn't stop Starkweather, who went into a bedroom and choked her two-year-old sister to death. He stashed the bodies outside, one in the chicken coop, another in an outhouse, and the baby's in a cardboard box.

Knowing someone might stop by, the two put up a note saying, "Stay a Way. Every Body is Sick With the Flu," and tacked it to the door.

A short time later, Caril Ann's older sister did in fact stop by and offer to help the "sick" family. Caril Ann turned her away, but the sister became suspicious and called the police, who came to investigate. Caril Ann managed to convince them that the family had the Asian flu, however, and they left.

Two days later, Caril Ann's grandmother visited, and she too was sent away. Not satisfied, she too called the police. This time the house was empty when they stopped by, so they left again.

Starkweather and Fugate had packed and taken off, marking their path with a deadly trail of bodies. Starkweather quickly killed two young strangers who stopped to help him when his car got stuck in the mud. He killed a friend for guns and ammunition.

In Lincoln, the dangerous duo entered the home of wealthy businessman C. Lauer Ward and proceeded to tie up Ward's wife and maid. Starkweather stabbed the women to death, then shot Ward when he showed up later.

By this time, the bodies at the Fugate home had been discovered and an alert was put out for Starkweather. More than one thousand police mobilized for the search.

Meanwhile, Starkweather and Fugate had stolen one of Ward's cars and were heading west. Outside the small town of Douglas, Wyoming, they came upon a salesman snoozing in his car at the side of the road. Starkweather fired once into the car, pulled the dazed man out, and shot him nine more times, killing him.

They hopped into the victim's car for the getaway, but Starkweather had a hard time releasing the parking brake. Passerby Joseph Sprinkle

AP/Wide World Photos

Caril Fugate and Charles Starkweather

stopped to help and Starkweather leveled his rifle at him. Sprinkle grabbed for the rifle just as a squad car pulled up with a deputy sheriff inside.

Starkweather screamed for Caril Ann to help him. Instead, she yelled to the policeman, "Help! It's Starkweather! He's going to kill me! He's crazy! Arrest him!"

Starkweather jumped into Sprinkle's car and tore away, but was stopped by a shotgun blast that blew out the windshield and grazed his head.

With guns aimed at him, Starkweather surrendered.

In the post-spree trial, Starkweather insisted that he had killed everyone in self-defense. He attempted to defend Fugate until she turned on him to save herself. Then Starkweather said that the girl had been a willing accomplice. She could have escaped numerous times when he left the car to get something to eat, leaving her with all the weapons.

Starkweather was found guilty and sentenced to death. He died in the electric chair in 1959.

Fugate, who proclaimed her innocence to the end, was sentenced to life in prison. She was paroled in 1977.

Date: April 4, 1958
Site: Beverly Hills, California
Type: Self-defense
Murderer: Cheryl Crane
Victim: Johnny Stompanato

....

THE WHOLE NATION listened to her story, but no one seemed to know if
Lana Turner was telling the truth. After all, she was an actress, and the
stakes here were bigger than an Academy Award—the freedom of her
fourteen-year-old daughter.

Turner had been called to testify at an inquest into the death of her
lover, Johnny Stompanato, described in the more flattering accounts as a
gigolo and small-time gangster.

Turner's daughter, Cheryl, from her marriage to Stephen Crane, had
witnessed an argument between Turner and Stompanato in the bedroom
of Turner's Beverly Hills home, during which Stompanato threatened,
not for the first time, to harm Turner.

"I'll cut you up and I'll get your daughter. . . . That's my business!"
said Stompanato according to Turner's testimony.

Cheryl, who had been listening in the next room, then ran to the
kitchen and picked up a nine-inch butcher knife. She opened the door to
see the man swing a jacket at her mother.

As Turner testified, "Everything happened so quickly that I did not
even see the knife in my daughter's hand. I thought she had hit him in the
stomach with her fist. Mr. Stompanato stumbled forward, turned around
and fell on his back. He choked, his hands on his throat. I ran to him and
lifted up his sweater. I saw the blood . . . . He made a horrible noise in
his throat."

Turner phoned her mother and her attorney for help. Doctors were
called as well, but it was too late. Stompanato had died on the spot.
Turner's tried to deflect blame from her daughter, but an inquest was
held.

Meanwhile, the media had a field day. They dug into the relationship
between Turner and thirty-two-year-old Stompanato, who was six years
her junior. The aging actress, whose discovery at a soda fountain on
Sunset Boulevard in the 1930s sparked one of Hollywood's most endur-
ing fantasies, had found her career slipping of late.

The relationship was one of many for Turner, whose fourth marriage,
to Lex Barker (an actor who had played Tarzan in the movies) had re-

cently ended. Stompanato had called Turner on a bet, thus beginning a year-long relationship that was often filled with threats of violence.

The inquest revealed much about the stormy relationship. The media revealed even more by printing some steamy love letters the pair had exchanged. (The letters were acquired from Mickey Cohen, a known mob figure, a friend of Stompanato's.)

In the end, Cheryl Crane's actions were ruled justifiable homicide, and she was freed.

And Lana Turner's career was rejuvenated.

AP/Wide World Photos

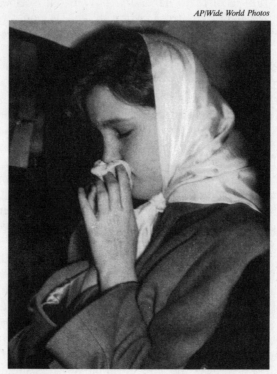

Cheryl Crane

Date: November 15, 1959

Site: Holcomb, Kansas

Type: Robbery

Murderers: Richard Hickock and Perry Smith

Victims: 4 members of the Clutter family

....

OF ALL THE MURDERS dramatized by the media, perhaps none is more famous than the slaughter of the Clutter family, the subject of Truman Capote's book *In Cold Blood* and a later movie with the same name starring Robert Blake and Scott Wilson.

The real-life murderers were Richard Hickock, twenty-eight, and Perry Smith, thirty-one. It was Hickock who hatched the plot to rob the Clutters, well-to-do farmers in Holcomb, Kansas. While in the Kansas State Penitentiary, Hickock had heard about the family from his cellmate, Floyd Wells, who had once worked for them.

Hickock pumped Wells for information about the family's fortune. Did they keep cash at home? Did they have a safe?

After his release from prison, Hickock joined with Smith to rob the farmers. Their disappointment at finding only fifty dollars in cash prompted a murder spree in which they cut the throat of Herbert Clutter, forty-five, and shot him in the head. Clutter's forty-five-year-old wife, Bonnie, his sixteen-year-old daughter, Nancy, and his fifteen-year-old son, Kenyon, were each bound by the wrists and shot at close range with a shotgun.

The murders made headlines all over the country. One particularly interested reader was Floyd Wells, who was still in the penitentiary. He went to prison authorities and told them of Hickock's interest in Clutter's financial situation. Hickock and Smith were then traced to Las Vegas, where they were arrested.

Both men were quick to confess. Hickock, however, said, "Perry Smith killed the Clutters. I couldn't stop him. He killed them all!"

And Smith had this to say of Herbert Clutter: "He was a nice gentleman. . . . I thought so right up to the moment I cut his throat."

After all appeals were exhausted, the killers were hanged in 1965.

Date: February 9, 1960 (approximate)

Site: Morrison, Colorado

Type: Kidnapping

Murderer: Joseph Corbett, Jr.

Victim: Adolph Coors III

••

MONEY HAS ITS PRIVILEGES. It also has its problems. For example, in the 1960s, the crime of kidnapping put many rich Americans at risk. One of these was forty-five-year-old Adolph Coors III, chairman of the board of the Coors Brewery in Golden, Colorado.

On the morning of February 9, 1960, Coors's station wagon was found empty, with its motor running, on a small bridge at the foot of the Rocky Mountains. Coors, whose family was among the wealthiest in the state, had left his nearby home several hours earlier.

The next day, Coors's wife received a ransom note, demanding $500,000 in cash. She was told to place a classified ad in the local paper to signal that she had it ready. The note concluded with this warning: "Adolph's life is in your hands. We have no desire to commit murder. All we want is that money. If you follow the instructions, he will be released unharmed within 48 hours after the money is received."

The Coors family cooperated, raising the money and placing the ad, which ran for several weeks without an answer.

Meanwhile, the FBI was on the case. Residents in the area where the abandoned car was found reported noticing several vehicles in the area at the time of Coors's disappearance. One of these was a 1951 yellow Mercury. The Bureau traced the car to Walter Osborne, who had lived in Denver until February 10 when he suddenly left town.

Osborne had taken out an insurance policy naming Joseph Corbett, Sr., of Seattle, as beneficiary. Agents in Seattle learned that Corbett had a son, Joseph Jr., whose physical description matched Osborne's.

Joseph Jr. had been convicted on a second-degree murder charge in California but had escaped from the prison where he was serving his sentence. As it turned out, his fingerprints matched those on a driver's license application filed by Osborne.

The FBI soon located the yellow Mercury in Atlantic City, New Jersey. Samples of soil taken from its fenders matched soil in Colorado, very near the scene of the kidnapping.

Months went by and the kidnappers made no further contact with the Coors family. Then, on September 11, 1960, someone found a pair of trousers lying on the ground on a mountainside south of Denver. In the pants was a penknife with the initials, AC III.

An intensive search of the area by police turned up a tie clasp, a pair of shoes, a wristwatch, and several articles of clothing that belonged to Coors.

They also found bones—animal bones and human bones. Dental records identified the skull as Coors's. Two .38 caliber bullet holes were found in a shoulder blade.

The FBI put Joseph Corbett, Jr., on its Ten Most Wanted list, and the November issue of *Reader's Digest* magazine featured a long account of the kidnapping and a picture of the fugitive.

The article produced a phone call from a Toronto resident who told local police that Corbett had lived nearby for several months but had recently moved, leaving no forwarding address. Then a Winnipeg resident called to say Corbett had lived there. At last, FBI agents traced him to a hotel in Vancouver, where he was captured without a fight.

Corbett was tried, convicted, and sentenced to life in prison. He was paroled one day in 1979 but rearrested the next for violating parole in California. He spent another year in prison before being released to a halfway house in 1980.

Date: June 1962 through January 1964

Site: Boston, Massachusetts

Type: Mass

Murderer: Albert DeSalvo

Victims: 13 women

HIS REAL NAME is almost forgotten now, but his nickname endures: "The Boston Strangler."

Albert DeSalvo's murderous string began on June 14, 1962, with the murder of fifty-five-year-old Anne Slesers. He beat her, raped her, and strangled her.

There were three more victims in June, another two in August, then two in December, four altogether in 1963, and one more, the last one, in January 1964. The women ranged in age from nineteen to eighty-five.

In most of these cases, the killer talked his way into the victim's home or apartment. Almost always, he strangled the woman, leaving a signature bow under her chin.

AP/Wide World Photos

Albert DeSalvo

After the January 1964 murder, the crimes suddenly ended. Authorities were baffled. They had no suspects until October 27, 1964. Early that morning, a woman sleeping in her Cambridge apartment was confronted by a man who tied her to the bed and molested her. "Don't look at me," he said, but she did. He left without further harming her, saying, "I'm sorry."

The woman gave police a description, and the police sketch was identified as Albert DeSalvo.

DeSalvo was defended by F. Lee Bailey, the well-known criminal lawyer, and found mentally incompetent to stand trial. The attorney argued that DeSalvo had "one of the most crushing sexual drives psychiatry has ever encountered. For a period of eighteen months, thirteen acts of homicide were committed by a completely uncontrollable vegetable walking around in a human body."

DeSalvo eventually was sentenced to life imprisonment for other crimes. He was stabbed to death by fellow inmates in 1973.

Date: August 28, 1962
Site: San Jose, California
Type: Torture
Murderer: Dr. Geza de Kaplany
Victim: Hajna de Kaplany

··

IT WAS CALLED nothing less than "the most horrendous single murder in American history." And its perpetrator was neither drug addict nor sex fiend, but a licensed doctor of anesthesiology.

The victim was the doctor's wife, Hajna de Kaplany, a part-time model described as one of the most beautiful women in the Hungarian community of San Jose, California.

Her husband, Dr. Geza de Kaplany, was said to be insanely jealous. To make sure his wife would never be desired by another man, Dr. de Kaplany decided to disfigure her. He stocked their apartment with bottles of nitric, hydrochloric, and sulfuric acid, rubber gloves, and adhesive tape.

Turning up the music on his radio, he tied his wife to their bed, cut her skin, and then poured acid into the wounds. Despite the loud music, neighbors heard her piteous cries. When the police came they found Hajna suffering horribly from third-degree burns—burns that later proved fatal.

At the murder trial that followed, de Kaplany pleaded not guilty by reason of insanity, claiming he had a "one-hour crack-up" and that he had only wanted to ruin his wife's looks, not kill her. But he was convicted and sentenced to life in prison anyway.

Although he was designated "a special interest prisoner," unlikely ever to be paroled, de Kaplany was paroled in 1976, after thirteen years in jail. He was sent to Taiwan to a missionary hospital in need of a doctor. His release, which was inadequately explained, is one of the most controversial in California history.

Date: June 12, 1963

Site: Jackson, Mississippi

Type: Racial

Murderer: Unknown

Victim: Medgar Evers

....

THE SHOT THAT KILLED civil rights activist Medgar Evers could still be heard nearly thirty years after his death, as the third trial of a suspect was to be held in late 1991.

Evers, thirty-seven, was a field secretary for the Mississippi branch of the National Association for the Advancement of Colored People. His life was threatened often during that time of voter registration drives and other civil rights activities in the South, but he was undaunted.

On June 12, 1963, after a meeting with NAACP lawyers, Evers arrived home at 12:30 A.M. As he walked from his car to his house he was shot in the back. The bullet went through his body—police later found it inside the house—but he staggered back towards his car before he fell, next to his station wagon, in the carport. His wife and three children ran to help him, but it was too late.

All over America, people were outraged by the cold blooded killing. President John F. Kennedy said he was "appalled by the barbarity."

Byron De la Beckwith, a resident of Signal Mountain, Tennessee, was arrested and tried, twice, for the killing in 1964, but both times the all-white juries ended up deadlocked. Eventually the murder charges were dropped.

This was not the end of the story, however. In 1989, a series of newspaper stories revealed that a segregationist agency was responsible for polling the jury, indicating that there may have been jury tampering. And a Ku Klux Klansman turned FBI informant provided some new evidence in the case.

De la Beckwith was arrested again in 1990 at the age of seventy. He spent ten months in a Tennessee jail fighting extradition, but in October 1991, he was sent to Mississippi after a judge rejected requests for court orders that would have blocked his return.

De la Beckwith maintains he is not guilty of the crime.

Date: July 30, 1963 and August 28, 1965

Site: Middletown, New Jersey, and Sarasota, Florida

Type: Poison

Murderer: Dr. Carl Coppolino

Victims: Colonel William Farber and Carmela Coppolino

WITH FAMED LAWYER F. Lee Bailey defending him, Dr. Carl Coppolino's trials on two charges of murder became national sensations. But unlike most of Bailey's cases, this one ended in defeat.

An anesthesiologist living with his wife in New Jersey, Coppolino retired at the age of thirty, claiming he had a heart ailment. His insurance company was suspicious but could find no reason not to pay him more than $20,000 a year in benefits.

Coppolino soon became friendly with neighbors Colonel William and Marjorie Farber, both in their fifties. Coppolino offered to help Mrs. Farber quit smoking through hypnotism. Instead, the two became intimate.

When Colonel Farber eventually became jealous of the relationship, Coppolino suggested to Mrs. Farber that they murder him. On July 3, 1963, Coppolino gave Farber an injection that was intended to kill him. When that didn't work, he placed a plastic bag over Farber's head, but Mrs. Farber interceded. Finally, Coppolino smothered the colonel with a pillow.

Coppolino told authorities that the death was due to heart failure, and because he was a physician they believed him.

Two years later, the Coppolinos moved to Sarasota, Florida. After a time, Mrs. Farber followed them there. But Dr. Coppolino had already taken up with a younger woman.

Dr. Coppolino asked his wife for a divorce, but she refused him. Then on August 28, 1965, Coppolino called a local doctor to report that his wife had died of a heart attack. Again, his judgment was trusted, and Mrs. Coppolino was buried with no embarrassing questions asked.

However when Mrs. Farber heard of Mrs. Coppolino's untimely demise, she went to the authorities and they exhumed the bodies of both Colonel Farber and Mrs. Coppolino.

A puncture mark was found on the late woman's buttock. According to the prosecution, the doctor had injected the drug succinylcholine into his wife, thereby causing a paralysis of the nervous system and a death that appeared to be from heart problems.

Represented by Bailey, Dr. Coppolino was acquitted in the Farber trial. Accounts at the time said that conflicting medical testimony had confused the jury.

The second trial was another matter altogether. Several medical experts clearly testified that Mrs. Coppolino had received an injection into her buttock. Another expert contended that while succinic acid, one of the components of the drug succinylcholine, is found in every body, the chemical found in Mrs. Coppolino's body was of the store-bought variety.

The doctor was judged guilty and sent to prison for life.

Not used to losing, Bailey lashed out at the prosecution and witnesses and was suspended from practicing law in the state of New Jersey for one year.

Date: August 28, 1963

Site: New York City

Type: Sex

Murderer: Richard Robles

Victims: Janice Wylie and Emily Hoffert

··

IT WAS A MURDER that was later to inspire a best-selling novel turned movie, an even more famous Supreme Court case, and a true-crime book.

The crime began as a simple burglary and turned into a brutal double murder with sexual overtones.

The victims were Janice Wylie, the twenty-one-year-old daughter of author Max Wylie and niece of author Philip Wylie, and her roommate, twenty-three-year-old Emily Hoffert.

Their bodies were found in their Manhattan apartment, tied together. Janice was nude; Emily, still dressed. Both women had been stabbed to death.

Eight months later, the police made a breakthrough that they felt solved the crime. They charged George Whitmore, Jr., who was currently a suspect in a rape and another murder, and he confessed. Later, however, Whitmore claimed that the police had forced the confession from him, beating him unmercifully until he finally told them what he thought they wanted to hear.

In January 1965, a year and a half after the murders, the police were able to tape-record conversations involving Richard Robles, a twenty-year-old addict and burglar whose statements led to his arrest and Whitmore's release. Robles was eventually found guilty of the two murders and sentenced to life in prison, although he never confessed.

Whitmore's case was referred to in the Supreme Court decision of Ernesto Miranda, in which the court ruled that a defendant's rights take effect the moment he or she is brought into custody.

The Wylie-Hoffert murders became the subject of a nonfiction book, *The Victims,* by Bernard Lefkowitz and Kenneth Gross, and was said to be among the sources for Judith Rossner's novel, *Looking for Mr. Goodbar.*

Date: November 22, 1963
Site: Dallas, Texas
Type: Assassination
Murderer: Lee Harvey Oswald
Victim: President John F. Kennedy

Date: November 24, 1963
Site: Dallas, Texas
Type: Revenge
Murderer: Jack Ruby
Victim: Lee Harvey Oswald

EXCEPT FOR THE assassination of Abraham Lincoln (see page 7), no murder in American history has been as debated, discussed, studied, and mourned as that of President John F. Kennedy.

All solid evidence points to these facts: on November 22, 1963, Kennedy was in Dallas, riding in a motorcade with his wife, Jackie, and Governor John B. Connally of Texas and his wife, on a route that had been publicized days in advance. At approximately 12:30 P.M., as the car passed in front of the Texas School Book Depository, three rapid shots rang out. Kennedy was hit by a bullet in the back of the neck, which exited the front, and by another that struck in the back portion of his head, causing a massive and fatal wound. One of the bullets that struck the President also hit Connally in the back, exited his chest, and hit his wrist and thigh.

Kennedy was rushed to Parkland Hospital where he was pronounced dead.

The killer, Lee Harvey Oswald, was an employee of the book depository. He had fired from a sixth-floor window, and then hid the high-powered Mannlicher-Carcano rifle between some cartons on the floor.

Oswald was questioned once by the police in the depository, but was allowed to leave. On the street, he was confronted by a Dallas policeman, J. D. Tippitt, about forty-five minutes after the shooting. Oswald shot and killed Officer Tippitt in front of many witnesses.

The police were later called to a movie theater where a man had entered without a ticket. The man was Oswald.

Two days after his arrest, Oswald himself was murdered. In front of millions, on national television, Jack Ruby shot him as he was being transferred to another jail. Ruby, a Dallas nightclub operator and an ardent admirer of the President, was convicted of Oswald's murder and imprisoned. He died early in 1967 of cancer.

With confusing evidence provoking a storm of controversy in the case, a special commission headed by Supreme Court Chief Justice Earl Warren investigated the assassination. The commission then issued a report which said it was satisfied that Oswald, acting alone, had killed Kennedy. Yet even today many people remain skeptical about the case.

Some theorists think that other gunmen fired at the same time as Oswald and then involved Ruby in a conspiracy to keep Oswald from talking. Since some of the evidence in the case remains sealed, many people believe that the definitive account of Kennedy's death is yet to come.

Why did Oswald kill the president?

No one knows for sure, but the Warren Commission pointed to his deep-rooted resentment of all authority, his inability to enter meaningful relationships, his urge to try to find a place in history, his capacity for violence, and his avowed commitment to Marxism.

Date: March 13, 1964

Site: Kew Gardens, New York

Type: Stabbing

Murderer: Winston Moseley

Victim: Kitty Genovese

....

FEW CRIMES IN American history have left more people feeling guilty than the murder of twenty-eight-year-old Kitty Genovese. On March 13, 1964, Genovese was attacked by a twenty-nine-year-old factory worker named Walter Moseley near her home in a heavily residential area in the New York City borough of Queens. As she was being stabbed over and over again, Kitty cried out to neighbors, screaming: "Oh, my God, he stabbed me! Please help me! Please help me!"

Windows went up all along the block. But the most anyone did was yell, "Let that girl alone." No one came out to help.

Moseley simply walked away. He returned a short time later to find Genovese desperately trying to make it to her home and stabbed her again. Once more she cried out, "I'm dying! I'm dying!" And still no one even called the police.

Again Moseley left, and again he returned to stab her one more time. When she was finally dead, he drove off.

In all, thirty-five minutes had elapsed from the first to the final attack.

Days later, police apprehended Moseley, who confessed to the murders of Genovese and two others. He was convicted and sentenced to life in prison.

When asked why no one had helped Kitty Genovese, her neighbors typically responded, "We didn't want to get involved."

Date: June 21, 1964

Site: Pennsylvania, Mississippi

Type: Racial

Murderer: Unknown

Victims: Michael Schwerner, Andrew Goodman,
James Chaney

....

IT TOOK FORTY-FOUR DAYS to uncover the missing bodies of the three civil rights workers whose burned out station wagon was found several miles north of Philadelphia, Mississippi. Their disappearance came during "Mississippi Summer" 1964, when a group of young civil rights workers mounted an ambitious voter registration drive among rural blacks in the South.

The search for the three—Michael Schwerner, twenty-four, and Andrew Goodman, twenty, were white men from New York City, and James Chaney, twenty-one, was a black man from Meridian, Mississippi—included marines and sailors from the Meridian Naval Air Station. Allen Dulles, former director of the Central Intelligence Agency, was sent to Mississippi on a fact-finding mission by President Lyndon Johnson shortly after the three disappeared. But it took a tip from an informer to point FBI agents to a farm in the area, where, under fifteen feet of dirt, the bodies of the three were buried. They had been shot to death.

According to the prosecution, Cecil Ray Price, the former deputy sheriff in Philadelphia, had arrested the three civil rights workers on the night of June 21, 1964. Chaney was held for speeding, the other two for something called "investigation."

Price released all three at about 10:30 P.M., ordering them to get out of town. But as soon as they were let go, they were chased by people in several cars and forced off the road some fifteen miles outside of town.

Price took them into custody again, and began driving them toward Philadelphia. But they never got there. Price suddenly stopped his car. The three young men were taken out of the car and shot at close range. Their bodies were brought to the farm and buried by a bulldozer.

While the federal government quickly began pointing to suspects, two indictments were dismissed in the courts on the basis of faulty procedures. Eventually, however, the Supreme Court upheld the federal government.

In October 1967, eighteen men were tried for conspiracy to deprive the three slain men of their rights under the Fourteenth Amendment to the Constitution, which guarantees due process.

After hearing testimony from one hundred and fifteen witnesses, the jury deliberated for one day and came back deadlocked. Judge Harold Cox sent them back to "carefully examine and reconsider" their positions.

The jury finally convicted seven. Among the guilty were Deputy Price; Samuel Bowers, a leader of the Ku Klux Klan; Alton Wayne Roberts, a former nightclub bouncer; Billy Wayne Posey, a service station operator; Jimmy Arledge and Jimmy Snowden, truck drivers; and Horace Doyle Barnette.

The jury remained deadlocked on three men, and mistrials were declared. Another eight men were acquitted.

Bowers and Roberts were sentenced to prison for ten years, Deputy Price and Posey for six years, while the other three received three-year sentences.

Date: July 14, 1965

Site: New York, New York

Type: Family

Murderer: Alice Crimmins

Victims: Edmund Crimmins, Jr., and Marie Crimmins

....

ALICE CRIMMINS, a cocktail waitress who was separated from her husband, called the New York City police in July 1965 to report that her five-year-old son and her four-year-old daughter were missing.

The next day, Marie was found, strangled, in an empty lot not far from where the family lived, in the borough of Queens. A few days later, Edmund was found too, but his body had decomposed so much it was impossible to determine the cause of his death.

Crimmins was charged with the death of her daughter soon afterward and convicted of manslaughter in a much-publicized trial in 1968. The conviction was overturned on appeal, however—when it was revealed that several jurors had visited the murder scene without the permission of the court.

Then, in 1971, Crimmins was tried again, this time for the murder of her son and for manslaughter in the death of her daughter. One witness testified that Crimmins had said she would "rather see her children dead" than with her husband, and the prosecution argued that she had killed the children to keep them from him. She was convicted of both crimes, but a higher court later reversed the murder conviction.

She began serving a sentence of five to twenty years. By 1977, Crimmins was participating in a work-release program, and she had been allowed to marry Anthony Grace, a wealthy building contractor. (Grace had testified at both trials that he was one of Crimmins's lovers.) She spent many of her weekend furloughs from prison on Grace's yacht. After five years in prison, Crimmins was paroled.

Date: July 16-17, 1966
Site: Chicago, Illinois
Type: Mass
Murderer: Richard Speck
Victims: 8 women

....

THE MAN SMELLED OF alcohol when he came to the door of the two-story townhouse at about midnight on July 16, 1966. His first words were polite. He merely needed some money to get to New Orleans. He wasn't going to harm anyone, but in his hands he held a knife and a gun.

Hours later, eight student nurses ranging in age from twenty-one to twenty-three were dead.

Richard Franklin Speck was born in Illinois but grew up in Texas. After sinking into a life filled with alcohol and drugs and serving time for forgery and assault, he went back to Illinois, supposedly in search of work.

On the night of the murders, he entered the nurses' Chicago home and tied them up. One of the nine young women who lived there managed to escape by crawling under a bunk bed. From her hideout, she could hear sounds of the massacre and occasionally catch a glimpse of Speck and his victims. Methodically, he took them either singly or in pairs to rooms around the house, where he sexually abused some, stabbed some, and strangled others during a nightmare period of several hours.

After the house finally grew silent at about 5 A.M., the nurse who had hidden under the bed climbed to a second-floor window ledge and began screaming "My friends are all dead! Help! Help! I'm the only one left alive!"

Police quickly put together a description of the suspect. They created a sketch based on the surviving nurse's description, and it was published in newspapers throughout the United States. The sketch and additional leads soon pointed to Richard Speck.

Around then, police were called to a downtown hotel where a man who had cut his wrist and arm was found lying in a pool of blood. Without knowing who he was, police took him to a local hospital. There, a doctor recognized Richard Speck's face from pictures published in the newspaper that day. His suspicions were confirmed when he found Speck's tattoo, which had been described in the paper. "Born to raise hell," it read.

Speck was arrested and charged with the murders. At his trial in 1967, the surviving nurse's testimony was key. It took the jurors only forty-nine minutes of deliberation to find Speck guilty. He was sentenced to death in the electric chair, but the verdict was changed to life in prison when the Supreme Court ruled that the death penalty was cruel and unusual punishment.

Speck died of an apparent heart attack at the age of 49 in December 1991. He was still in prison at the Stateville Correctional Center in Joliet, Illinois.

One of the bedrooms where Speck killed the nursing students

Date: August 1, 1966

Site: Austin, Texas

Type: Mass

Murderer: Charles Whitman

Victims: 15 people

···

IT IS COMMON PRACTICE, it seems, for reports of a sensational murder to paint the suspect in one of two ways: typically the person is either inherently evil or seems almost too good to be true.

Charles Whitman definitely belonged in the latter category.

He was tall and handsome, a hard-working student, a married man, a good hunter, even a former Marine and an Eagle Scout. Unfortunately, beneath his shining exterior Whitman had a darker side that only his close friends were able to discern.

On March 29, 1966, Whitman, then twenty-five years old, sought help from a psychiatrist at the University of Texas, where he was a student in engineering and a part-time summer worker.

Though he was only able to spend an hour with Whitman, the psychiatrist, like many of Whitman's friends, sensed inner turmoil. "This massive, muscular youth seemed to be oozing with hostility."

The psychiatrist's report went on to say that the precipitating factor for the visit was the split between Whitman's parents thirty days earlier. His father had been calling Charles every few days, urging him to talk his mother into returning.

The report also stated that Whitman had admittedly experienced overwhelming periods of hostility with very little provocation and had actually thought about "going up on the [University of Texas] tower with a deer rifle to start shooting people."

Although the psychiatrist did not sense any imminent danger, he asked Whitman to return in a week and gave him a phone number to call if he needed to talk before then. Whitman never called and he never came back.

But four months later, early on August 1, he drove to his mother's apartment, where he shot her in the back of the head and stabbed her in the chest. He left a note addressed, "To whom it may concern:

"I have just killed my mother. If there's a heaven, she's going there. If there's not a heaven, she is out of her pain and misery.

"I love my mother with all my heart."

Whitman returned home, and a few hours later he stabbed his sleeping wife in the chest three times, killing her. Again a note:

"At 3 A.M., both dead."

Four hours later, Whitman bought a shotgun at a department store, rented a dolly, and drove to the university, asking for a parking pass so he could deliver equipment to a campus building. At the tower, he asked a receptionist to help him pull the dolly laden with a footlocker, parcels, and a long, blanket-wrapped-bundle onto the elevator. The woman obliged.

When they reached the observation deck, 307 feet above the ground, Whitman bashed in the skull of the fifty-one-year-old receptionist before firing a shot into her head.

A young couple then bumped into Whitman, but he allowed them to leave. Just before noon, however, a family of sight-seers headed toward the tower and Whitman opened fire, killing several of them.

After blocking the door to the tower deck, he laid down his weapons—by one account three rifles, one shotgun, and two pistols—around the four sides of the deck. Then the firing resumed.

AP/Wide World Photos

Charles and Kathy Whitman, August 1962

Whitman, a deadly accurate marksman, fired for nearly ninety minutes. Among his victims:

- a seventeen-year-old paper carrier, shot in the groin;
- a twenty-two-year-old policeman, who was responding to the call of shots;
- a city electrical worker, who temporarily left his truck;
- a lifeguard and his sweetheart, both eighteen, who were walking hand in hand;
- a pregnant mother, shot in the stomach, who survived the assault but lost her baby.

Finally, a group of policemen slowly made their way to the deck and broke through Whitman's barricade. Officer Ramiro Martinez, twenty-nine at the time, took advantage of a distracting shotgun blast from another member of the party and emptied his service revolver into Whitman, who fell to the ground but continued to move. With a shotgun, Martinez then fired into Whitman's head and killed him.

In all, thirteen were dead, in addition to Whitman's wife and mother, and another thirty-one were wounded.

Later, authorities found yet another note written by Whitman, apparently just before his murder spree began: "I am prepared to die. After my death, I wish an autopsy on me to be performed to see if there's any mental disorder."

An autopsy did show a highly malignant brain tumor, but a relationship between the tumor and his actions was never clearly established.

Date: September 18, 1966

Site: Kenilworth, Illinois

Type: Unknown

Murderer: Unknown

Victim: Valerie Percy

....

SOME CASES REFUSE to be "officially" solved. The murder of Valerie Percy, one of the twin daughters of a wealthy industrialist and candidate for the U.S. Senate, appears to fit that category. For, despite more than ten thousand police interviews and over one thousand suspects, no charges were ever brought in the against anyone.

The crime occurred in the midst of Charles Percy's 1966 Senate campaign. With all the activity going on then, late-night noise in the Percy mansion in Kenilworth, Illinois, was not unusual. Percy and his wife, Lorraine, had returned home late Saturday night, watched TV for a while, and then retired.

Sometime during the night, Mrs. Percy later reported, she heard the sound of breaking glass, but she figured it was a water glass. At about 5 A.M., however, she was awakened by sounds of moaning coming from her twenty-one-year-old daughter Valerie's room. Inside Mrs. Percy saw a man standing over Valerie's bed. She ran back to her room and woke her husband, who pressed a burglar alarm and then ran to Valerie's room.

But the man had escaped down the stairs.

Valerie's skull had been crushed by repeated blows with what was probably a hammer. She had also been stabbed ten times in the abdomen, chest, and throat.

Few clues were apparent. Scores of interviews failed to reveal a motive for the murder.

After much agonizing, Percy decided to resume his campaign. He won the election.

While no one has ever been charged with the crime, authorities who investigated the murders feel certain that one of two suspects they uncovered in the process was the culprit.

Frederick Malchow, a cross-country career burglar, was the most likely. Malchow, who was interviewed by FBI agents while awaiting trial for another crime in Pennsylvania, later told a fellow inmate that he was nervous that a pair of trousers could get him into further trouble in the Percy case.

The trousers he referred to were eventually found by the police, but too much time had passed for any scientific analysis to connect them with the case. Further interviews with Malchow became impossible when he escaped from prison in 1967, then fell from a railroad trestle to his death as police hunted him.

Another suspect, who had worked with Malchow, died mysteriously in a fall from a thirty-story Chicago building.

Date: August 1967 to July 1969
Site: Michigan
Type: Serial sex
Murderer: Norman Collins
Victims: 7 women, aged 13 and up

••

WITH MORE THAN a bit of luck, Norman Collins almost got away with murder—seven times. But his luck finally ran out at the home of a relative, whose husband happened to be a state policeman.

Collins, a student at Eastern Michigan University, had been to his aunt's house several times to let the dog out during her family's vacation trip. When the family returned, the aunt's husband—a corporal in the state police—found splotches of fresh paint in the basement. Under the paint were brown stains that looked like blood.

The stains turned out to be varnish, but while searching the basement, police found hair clippings from haircuts the family gave in the basement. Matching hair clippings had turned up in evidence found in one of seven brutal slayings of young women in the Ypsilanti area, and Collins later admitted that he had "used" the basement during the family's absence. Other stains in the basement were indeed blood.

These discoveries, on July 29, 1969, and the resulting arrest of Collins wrapped up two years of unsolved murders in the area.

The victims:

• an Eastern Michigan student, who had been stabbed to death, her feet and hands hacked off;
• a twenty-year-old college student who had been raped and stabbed forty-seven times;
• another Eastern Michigan student, shot with a .22-caliber gun;
• a sixteen-year-old girl, known to police as a drug user, found beaten with a blunt instrument;
• a thirteen-year-old girl, found nearly naked and strangled;
• a partially clad university graduate, found stabbed and shot.

While much of the evidence presented at the trial was circumstantial, Norman Collins was convicted and sentenced to life in prison.

Date: April 4, 1968

Site: Memphis, Tennessee

Type: Assassination

Murderer: James Earl Ray

Victim: Dr. Martin Luther King, Jr.

James Earl Ray

··

JAMES EARL RAY was by all accounts only an average criminal, but he thought big. It was his ambition to make the Federal Bureau of Investigation's Most Wanted list.

On April 4, 1968, Ray did just that when he assassinated the leader of the civil rights movement in the United States, Nobel Peace Prize-winner, the Reverend Dr. Martin Luther King, Jr., as King stepped out onto the balcony of his room in the Lorraine Motel in Memphis, Tennessee.

Using a .30-caliber rifle, Ray fired only one shot. It hit King in the neck, passing through his lower jaw, severing his spinal column, and killing him within the hour.

After firing, Ray, already wanted for his escape months earlier from the Missouri State Penitentiary, jumped into a white Mustang and took off for Canada.

From Canada, he flew to Europe, where he was eventually arrested and returned to the United States. Avoiding a jury trial and possible death penalty, Ray pleaded guilty to a charge of first-degree murder, for which a ninety-nine-year sentence was likely to be imposed.

His sudden rush to justice fueled rumors of a conspiracy. Where, it was asked, did Ray, who was destitute, get the money to finance the assassination, especially the flights to Canada and to Europe?

That question has never been answered to the satisfaction of many. Meanwhile, Ray made the FBI's list a second time when he escaped from a federal prison in June 1977. But he was recaptured a short time later. In 1981, Ray was stabbed twenty-two times by fellow inmates, injuries from which he recovered.

Date: June 5, 1968

Site: Los Angeles

Type: Assassination

Murderer: Sirhan Sirhan

Victim: Robert F. Kennedy

··

THE WORDS ". . . and on to Chicago, and let's win there," echo hollowly in the history books. For shortly after he spoke them, Robert F. Kennedy lost his life.

Kennedy, a U.S. Senator and brother of President John F. Kennedy, was speaking to a group of supporters in the Los Angeles Ambassador Hotel in the early morning hours of June 5, 1968, following his victory in the California presidential primary.

After leaving the podium, Kennedy headed down the hallway to an exit flanked by supporters and bodyguards. Among them was Sirhan Sirhan, a twenty-four-year-old immigrant from Jordan, who suddenly dropped a poster he had in his hand, lifted a .22-caliber pistol, and fired several shots. One of them hit Kennedy in the head and killed him.

Sirhan was wrestled to the ground and taken into custody. In the hours that followed the shooting, Sirhan joked with police, asking that his coffee be tasted to ensure there was no poison in it and commenting on the Boston Strangler murders.

When they investigated his background, authorities found a scarred childhood in his native, strife-torn Jerusalem. They also found notebooks, filled with such statements as "RFK must die" and "My determination to eliminate RFK is becoming more and more of an unshakable obsession."

Graphic evidence of his involvement, including tape recordings and film of the scene, were introduced at his trial. Found guilty of first-degree murder, Sirhan Sirhan was sentenced to death but spared by the Supreme Court ruling. He remains in prison.

Date: August 8 and August 10, 1969

Site: Los Angeles

Type: Mass

Murderers: Charles Manson and his followers

Victims: 7 people

••

SHORTLY AFTER THE ARREST of Charles Manson and his "family" for seven murders, one youthful follower attempted to describe the leader's appeal by saying, "He simply overpowered you. It was the way he looked at you. His eyes did strange things. When Charlie talked, people listened."

Today, more than twenty years later, Manson's eyes remain intense, and he is still the subject of television interviews from prison now and then. It is doubtful those eyes will ever again see the freedom of the world outside, however.

Manson's crimes have been among the most publicized of any in United States history, spawning the best-selling book *Helter Skelter* and still attracting attention decades after they happened.

What distinguished the murders of seven individuals in the course of two days in 1969 was not only the victims' fame but the savage nature of the killings themselves.

The first was the most shocking. On August 9, 1969, four members of Manson's group (Manson was not with them) broke into the rented Beverly Hills estate of film director Roman Polanski and methodically shot, beat, and stabbed five people to death. The victims were Polanski's wife, actress Sharon Tate, twenty-six, who was eight-and-a-half months pregnant at the time; Jay Sebring, thirty-five, a prominent hair stylist; Wojiciech Frykowski, thirty-seven, a friend of Polanski's; Abigail Folger of the Folger's coffee family, twenty-six, a friend of Frykowski's, and Steven Parent, eighteen, a friend of the estate's caretaker.

One of the accused later described the scene: "One man had a gun; the girls had knives. They parked the car so they could get away quickly. A man with wire cutters went up a pole and cut utility lines outside the Tate house. They saw Parent starting to leave. He got into his car and was shot. A man went through an open window, then opened the front door. The others went inside. Frykowski was lying on the couch. Sharon Tate and Sebring were talking in her bedroom. The Folger girl was in another bedroom, reading a book. Tate and Sebring were told to stay in the bedroom. Then they were brought out. Miss Tate became very apprehensive.

Charles Manson

"She wanted to make sure her baby was not harmed. That was virtually all she pleaded for, 'Let me have my baby.' But she was killed. Sebring said very little. He was killed. Frykowski attempted to escape. As he ran through the front door he was hit on the head with a gun butt. Miss Folger handed them all the money she had, seventy-three dollars, and they took it and killed her and Frykowski anyway."

The killers wrote slogans on walls and doors, some with the blood of the victims, two of whom were tied together.

Two nights later, with no viable suspects, police added another bizarre crime to the mystery when Leno LaBianca, a wealthy supermarket owner, and his wife, Rosemary, were killed in a similar manner just ten miles from where the Tate murders occurred.

Months went by without a break in the case. Then, some 350 miles from the death scenes, police raided a "hippie commune" in Death Valley, arresting Manson and members of his "family"—who were arrested for auto theft. One of the women made reference to the Tate murder, and she was transferred to a jail separate from the others. There, she began confiding in her cellmate details of the murders that could have only been known by someone who was there.

As a result of this information, indictments for murder were eventually brought against Manson, Charles Watson, Pat Krenwinkel, Linda Kasabian, and Sue Atkins. Although Manson had not actually participated in the murders, he was accused of ordering them.

Court proceedings stretched out over the next two years, with sentencing finally handed down in April 1970. Eventually, all the defendants were found guilty and sentenced to death in the gas chamber. They were given life imprisonment when the Supreme Court outlawed capital punishment.

At the time of the sentencing, however, the judge said the death penalty was not only appropriate, "but it is almost compelled by this case." He also said, "After nine-and-a-half months of trial all of the superlatives have been used. . . . All that remains are the bare, stark facts of seven senseless murders—seven people whose lives were snuffed out by total strangers for motives that remain known only to them."

Date: December 17, 1969

Site: Altamont, California

Type: Celebrity

Murderer: Unknown

Victim: Meredith Hunter

....

THE MURDER TOOK PLACE in front of an estimated 300,000 witnesses. Few who saw the incident actually realized what had happened.

The setting was a live rock concert by the Rolling Stones at the Altamont Speedway near San Francisco on December 17, 1969.

The concert was a hastily arranged event that had been switched from another site to the Altamont spot only days before. Security for the Stones and other groups playing that day were handled by one of the Stones' managers, who offered the Hells Angels motorcycle club a truckload of beer to keep the stage safe. Local police were not invited into the private arena.

One of the fans in attendance was eighteen-year-old Meredith Hunter from Berkeley. It was Hunter's body that was delivered cut and bleeding to the first-aid station at the concert. Doctors, however, were unable to help. He had been stabbed several times in the back.

Detectives assigned to the case were able to view thousands of feet of footage from a crew that had been there making a movie of the concert. On one reel of the movie, called *Gimme Shelter,* the murder itself was evident. Hunter had gotten into a confrontation with several of the Angels, who were swinging sawed-off billiard cues. After being knocked down, the youth had come up waving a revolver. A group of Angels had then descended and stabbed him to death.

Through witnesses who described the Angel who stabbed Hunter, and from the film itself, detectives were able to arrest twenty-one-year-old Alan David Passaro of San Jose, California. He was charged with the murder, but a jury acquitted him on grounds of self-defense.

Years later, in 1985, Passaro was found dead, drowned in a reservoir south of San Francisco. The police called the death suspicious, but no charges were brought against anyone.

Date: February 17, 1970

Site: Raleigh, North Carolina

Type: Family

Murderer: Jeffrey MacDonald

Victims: Colette, Kimberly, and Kristen MacDonald

··

TWENTY YEARS LATER, the *Fatal Vision* case continues to haunt America. For as of October 1990, more than twenty years after a crime that shocked the nation, attorneys for Jeffrey MacDonald, a Green Beret doctor convicted of killing his pregnant wife and their two children, were pressing for a new trial.

The attorneys claimed that evidence in the case had been suppressed by the government, evidence that would probably free MacDonald. Among the items attorneys said they had uncovered were forensic notes and testimony about an alleged confession by a one-time suspect in the case.

It all began on February 17, 1970, when military police were called to the home of MacDonald. There they found the Princeton-educated physi-

Jeffrey MacDonald

cian lying with his arm around his wife, Colette, twenty-six at the time; she was covered with blood, stabbed to death.

MacDonald moaned to the MPs to check his children. Their quick search turned up the bodies of Kimberly, age five, and Kristen, two, both dead.

MacDonald himself had several wounds, for which he was hospitalized. According to the story he told MPs and hospital personnel, four "acidheads" had come into his home—two white men, one black man, and a white woman with long blond hair who wore a floppy hat and held a candle. The woman kept chanting, "Acid is groovy," and "Kill the pigs."

Suspicion eventually fell on MacDonald himself, who in 1979 was tried, convicted, and sentenced to three consecutive life terms, the harshest punishment the judge could hand down. Among the most critical evidence presented during the trial was a fiber-and-blood reconstruction of the crime, as investigators had no witnesses.

In 1990, attorneys for MacDonald claimed that during the trial the government had not allowed the testimony of several people who had heard a "confession" from a one-time suspect in the case who claimed to have been involved in the murders. A chronic drug abuser, the woman had died in 1983. And though she wasn't blond she had said that she often wore blond wigs.

MacDonald cooperated with a book about his case, *Fatal Vision*, by Joe McGinniss which was turned into a television miniseries. But even as McGinniss was researching the book, he became convinced that MacDonald was guilty.

In July 1991, MacDonald's petition for a new trial was denied.

Date: 1970 to 1971

Site: Yuba City, California

Type: Mass

Murderer: Juan Corona

Victims: 25 men

....

IT HARDLY SEEMS POSSIBLE that twenty-five men could disappear over the course of a year and not be missed. Yet that is essentially what happened to the victims of Juan Corona, a handsome farm labor contractor and father of four.

The first of the bodies was found on May 21, 1970, when a worker on a ranch became aware of a newly dug hole. He later became suspicious when the hole was filled in, so he alerted the police.

A tractor driver discovered the second body buried in a mound.

A month of searching uncovered another twenty-three bodies. The victims had all been stabbed repeatedly in the chest, and their backs were hacked open in the shape of crosses. Authorities figured the bodies had been buried for anywhere from forty-eight hours to two months.

The victims ranged in age from forty to sixty-three. Most of them were drifters whom Corona had picked up with promises of work, and he then allegedly robbed them and then killed them.

Among the remains of several of the victims were receipts bearing Corona's name. A search of the suspect's house yielded the likely murder weapon, an 18-inch machete stained with blood and hair. Even more damning was the discovery of a "death list" with names of victims and inscribed dates after them.

Although he insisted that he knew nothing of the murders, Corona was found guilty of murder and sentenced to twenty-five consecutive life terms.

In 1973, Corona was attacked in prison and stabbed thirty-two times. As a result he lost the sight in one eye. He then suffered three heart attacks. And finally, his wife, who had stood by him throughout his original trial, divorced him.

In 1982, Corona was retried after an appeals court said that his lawyer had failed to call witnesses or explore Corona's mental capacity.

In the new trial, defense attorneys argued that the real killer was not Corona but his half-brother, Natividad, who had disappeared after Corona's arrest in 1971. He was believed to have died two years later of syphilis in Mexico. One witness testified that Natividad was a violent homosexual who had been seen slashing one of the twenty-five victims during a sex act in the back room of a café. The witness's credibility was diminished, however, when he later admitted he had lied about his occupation and background.

The verdict in this trial was no different than the first one: Corona was found guilty. Members of the jury later said that the death-list found in Corona's home had "tied it up for everyone."

According to reports, the seven-month retrial cost the state of California more than $5 million. The first trial had cost a mere $415,000.

Date: 1970 to 1973

Site: Houston, Texas

Type: Sex

Murderers: Dean Corll, Elmer Wayne Henley, David Brooks

Victims: 27 boys

··

AS THE GRIM TASK of unearthing bodies went on and on, Houston police became aware that they were closing in on the dubious record for the worst mass murder cases in United States history. When the final count was recorded, there were twenty-seven bodies.

All of the victims were young boys believed to have been tortured, sexually abused, and then killed by a thirty-three-year-old bachelor and his two young accomplices.

The killing stopped when one of the accomplices shot Dean Allen Corll to death during a paint-sniffing party, which involved seventeen-year-old Elmer Wayne Henley, a fifteen-year-old girl, and a twenty-year-old man. Henley called the police, and the grisly story began unraveling.

According to Henley, Corll had turned on him: "I remember waking up and Dean Corll was slapping handcuffs on me," Henley began. He then described how he had picked up a gun and pointed it at Corll. "I told Dean to back up and let those people up. He took a step toward me. I had the gun pointed at him. He said, 'You won't do it,' and came at me. I guess I shot him."

Bodies were found buried in several isolated sites that had never raised suspicions. Corll himself, who was considered a pleasant and quiet individual by his neighbors, had always seemed above suspicion.

Henley and David Brooks told the police how they had gotten their young victims drunk, then taken them to Corll, who tied them up and abused them, often taking as long as twenty-four hours to kill them off.

Henley received a 594-year sentence and Brooks, life in prison. In 1979, Henley won a new trial but was convicted again.

The case prompted newspapers around the country to decry the problem of runaways in the United States. As one newspaper editorial concluded, "We must not become so hardened that we dismiss every child who disappears as a runaway. The tragedy of Houston dramatizes that all too clearly."

Date: November 9, 1971

Site: Westfield, New Jersey

Type: Family

Murderer: John List

Victims: Helen, Patricia, John, Frederick, and Alma List

....

PEOPLE NOTICED THAT the lights were on day and night in the Westfield, New Jersey, home, but in this stately area of Victorian mansions people did not pry. When the lights began to go out one by one, however, one neighbor decided to call the police.

An officer came to investigate. When no one answered the door, he shone his flashlight through a window and made a horrible discovery: Neatly arranged in sleeping bags on the ballroom floor were the bodies of three teenaged children and an adult woman. The policeman also found an older woman's body stuffed into a closet upstairs.

The thermostat for the house was set at a very low temperature but despite the cold, the bodies had been decomposing for nearly a month, experts estimated. They were still identifiable, however, as members of the List family: John's wife, Helen, forty-six, his daughter, Patricia, sixteen, his sons John, fifteen, and Frederick, thirteen, and his mother, Alma, eighty-five. It was she who was found in the closet.

List himself had disappeared. But he had taken the precaution of informing the children's schools, and the post office, and a few others that the family was taking an extended vacation.

A nationwide search for List was begun, and his car was found, in a parking lot at Kennedy Airport in New York City. But List did not turn up.

Seventeen years passed. And then the List case was featured on the television show, "America's Most Wanted." Pictures of List taken around the time of the murders as well as a sculptor's projections of how he would look in 1988 were broadcast all over America.

A viewer recognized him. He was living under the name Robert P. Clark, in Newark, New Jersey, and he was arrested eleven days after the program aired. At first he denied that he was List, but the FBI matched his fingerprints to make the identification undeniable.

After killing his family, he had eaten a meal and cleaned the house. Then he zigzagged across the country by train, ending up in Denver, Colorado, where he spent most of the next seventeen years. He married in 1977 and eventually moved back to New Jersey, where he worked for an accounting firm.

List left a letter for the pastor of his church that said "At least I'm certain that all have gone to heaven now. If things had gone on, who knows if that would be the case." He also expressed concern about his daughter's desire to become an actress. "I was fearful as to what this might do to her continuing to be a Christian," he wrote.

List was convicted on all five counts of premeditated murder. He did not testify at his trial, but at his sentencing hearing he said, "I wish to inform the court I remain truly sorry for the tragic events of 1971. . . . I ask all affected by this for their forgiveness, understanding, and prayer."

He was sentenced to five consecutive life terms—the maximum possible penalty under the law.

Date: 1972 to 1978

Site: Knollwood Park Township, Illinois

Type: Serial

Murderer: John Wayne Gacy

Victims: 33 young boys and men

....

You can't judge a book by its cover, the saying goes. It might also be said that you can't judge a clown by his smile, or a man by his good deeds. John Wayne Gacy certainly proved the last two true.

For over six years, Gacy preyed on thirty-three young boys and men, sexually attacking and killing them, then burying most of them in the crawlspace of his home in Knollwood Park Township, a suburb of Chicago.

At the time the bodies were discovered, Gacy was living an ostensibly wholesome life, operating a remodeling business in the area and even donning a clown costume to perform for young children.

In fact, his background was filled with outstanding public service. While living in Iowa during the 1960s, he was the chaplain of the Jaycees chapter, a position at which he was said to have excelled. He spent hours working on charitable projects.

But it was also in Iowa that Gacy was arrested for engaging in sexual activities with some of the young boys he hired to work in his fried chicken restaurant. Convicted of sodomy in 1968, he was sentenced to the Iowa State Reformatory for ten years.

After serving a short time, during which he worked on a Jaycees chapter for the prison, he was released for good behavior and moved to Chicago. There, in 1971, he was arrested again for attempting to have sexual relations with a young boy. But the youth failed to show up for the trial and the charges were dropped.

Gacy married while in Chicago, but the marriage broke up in 1976, shortly after he started a contracting business.

It was the business that eventually led to his arrest, connecting him as it did to one of his last victims.

The boy, a fifteen-year-old, had asked his mother to pick him up at the drug store where he was then working. When she arrived, however, he told her to wait in the car "for a few minutes" while he went to talk to a man about a better-paying construction job. He never came back. The mother drove home and called the police.

When the youth was still missing the next day, police began checking for clues to his disappearance. Among the leads they checked into was that of a contractor who had done some repair work at the drug store where the boy worked. The owner of the drug store confirmed that the contractor, whose work crew included a large number of young boys, had offered the boy a job.

The contractor, of course, was Gacy. Initially, he denied knowing anything about the missing boy. But police found a receipt belonging to the youth in Gacy's home. Armed with a warrant to search Gacy's home, police got him to admit he had indeed killed the boy—in self-defense, Gacy said.

Eventually, Gacy led the police to a concrete floor, under which he said the body was buried. But that was just the beginning. In a crawlspace beneath Gacy's house, police found the most horrific burial grounds in American history with dozens of victims. Most of them had been buried in two-foot trenches, then covered with lime to speed their deterioration.

And still there were more.

While most of the victims were found on the Gacy property, which was quickly reduced to rubble as the digging continued, others—including the youngster who never returned to his mother's car—were found in a local river.

Judged to be sane at the time of the murders, Gacy was convicted of thirty-three murders and sentenced to die in the electric chair. A 1983 interview showed an unrepentant Gacy, who continued to claim he had not been involved in the murders. "Where the hell could I have found time for all the things I was accused of?" he said. "I was working sixteen hours a day, and the rest of my time was devoted to the community, charity affairs, and helping young people."

He held to the belief that he would never be executed.

A lengthy appeal process seemed ended when the U.S. Supreme Court rejected arguments against the sentence in May of 1989.

However, he is still awaiting his fate.

Date: December 1, 1973

Site: Detroit, Michigan

Type: Kidnap

Murderers: Byron Smith, Geary Gilmore, Jerome Holloway

Victims: Gerald Craft, Keith Arnold

••

IT HAS BECOME KNOWN as the black Lindbergh case. On December 1, 1973, two black youngsters, aged eight and six, were kidnapped while playing in front of their homes.

After a ransom note demanding $53,000 was forwarded to the police, they attempted to win the youngsters' release by setting up a drop, using paper instead of money. But they were unable to capture anyone.

Several days later, the bodies of Gerald Craft, eight, and Keith Arnold, six, were found in two different fields. Each child had been shot in the head. Gerald Craft had been the star of a popular Kentucky Fried Chicken commercial. Keith was his friend.

Within weeks, three men were arrested. Byron Smith, Geary Gilmore, and Jerome Holloway were later convicted of the crime, and each received a life sentence.

Date: 1974 through 1978

Site: Washington, Utah, Colorado, and Florida

Type: Serial

Murderer: Theodore Bundy

Victims: 36 to 100 women

••

IT CAN BE extremely misleading when handsome actors are allowed to play real-life murderers in motion pictures. But in the case of Theodore Bundy, the casting would have been accurate.

Below the surface of a man most often described as romantically appealing raged the ugly truth: Ted Bundy, one of America's most horrific criminals, took lives of an uncountable number—estimates range from thirty-six to one hundred women—in a multi-year killing spree.

Bundy, who aspired to be a lawyer, ended up in court with only one client—himself. But there was no possible defense for the mountain of evidence against him.

Bundy's string of murders, lasting many years, began in his home state of Washington, where the bodies of nine women were found. Most of the victims had been sexually assaulted and either bludgeoned or strangled. It continued in Utah with six more bodies, and Colorado with another three.

Bundy was finally caught in Florida, but only after he had attacked yet another six more women, three of whom later died. Five of the attacks occurred on a single evening, January 15, 1978, four at a sorority house on the campus of Florida State University in Tallahassee. A fifth occurred the same night in an apartment only blocks away.

While police collected evidence, including bite marks on several of the victims, weeks went by without a break. Finally, a police officer on a routine patrol spotted a suspicious-looking automobile and stopped the driver. When he discovered that the vehicle was stolen, the policeman began to handcuff the driver, only to have him break free and run. The officer drew his gun and fired a warning shot. The man stopped and was taken into custody.

In attempting to learn the suspect's identity, police came across a poster from the Federal Bureau of Investigation's Ten Most Wanted program. Their unnamed prisoner was none other than fugitive Theodore Robert Bundy, who was being sought "for a 1975 murder at a ski resort near Aspen, Colorado."

The poster went on to say that "Bundy, who has been convicted of aggravated kidnapping, was awaiting trial for this murder when he escaped from a Colorado jail on December 31, 1977. In addition, he is wanted for questioning in connection with thirty-six similar sexual slayings that took place throughout several Western states."

Bundy was eventually convicted of three murders, all in the state of Florida. One of those victims was twelve-year-old Kimberly Leach of Lake City, whose body was found in a state park. Her death was attributed to "violence in the neck region."

For these crimes, Theodore Bundy was sentenced to death. He was sent to the electric chair on January 24, 1989, at the age of forty-two.

Before he died, Bundy blamed the widespread influence of pornography, TV violence, and X-rated movies for his behavior.

FBI

Theodore Bundy

Date: 1975
Site: Ann Arbor, Michigan
Type: Poisoning
Murderer: Unknown
Victims: 8 people

DURING THE SUMMER OF 1975, there were nearly fifty cases of respiratory arrest at the Veterans Administration Hospital in Ann Arbor, Michigan, several of which resulted in death.

Because the facility was under the jurisdiction of the federal government the FBI was called in to investigate. Months later, nurses Filipina Narcisco and Leonora Perez were charged with attempting to poison patients.

Prosecutors alleged that the two nurses had introduced a quick-acting muscle relaxant called Pavulon into the intravenous lines of patients in the hospital's intensive care unit. The drug—an overdose of which can cause suffocation—was kept under lock and key in the hospital, with access reserved for staff, according to authorities.

Although they had access to the drug, the case against the nurses was anything but open and shut. First of all no motive for the murders was ever uncovered. And then, almost as soon as the indictments against the pair of nurses were released, a Detroit newspaper reported that the nurses' former supervisor had left a note before her death exonerating them.

Nevertheless, in July 1977, the two were found guilty in federal court, but they were not sentenced.

Later that year another federal judge overturned the verdict and granted a new trial to the nurses, claiming they had been the victims of courtroom improprieties and circumstantial evidence.

The decision, announced on December 20, prompted Perez to say, "It's a great relief. We haven't had any good Christmases the past two years. Now we will."

Two months later the government announced it had dropped all charges against the women and would not proceed with a new trial.

The nurses were freed and the case has yet to be solved.

Date: July 30, 1975

Site: Detroit, Michigan

Type: Organized Crime

Murderer: Unknown

Victim: Jimmy Hoffa

....

THE MURDER OF Jimmy Hoffa, a former leader of the Teamsters Union, who disappeared on July 30, 1975, is considered one of the greatest mysteries in the annals of crime. Not only was his killer never found, but almost two decades after he was last seen alive, his body still has not been found.

What really happened to Hoffa? Was he murdered, and if so, how? Why? And by whom?

At the time of his disappearance sixty-two-year-old Jimmy Hoffa was in the process of trying to regain the leadership of the labor union he had been forced out of in the 1960s when he became a target of then Attorney General Robert F. Kennedy. While Hoffa's trial for demanding and receiving illegal payments ended with a hung jury, he had been found guilty not only of misappropriating Teamster funds but attempting to bribe one of the jurors. He was given a sentence of eight years.

Hoffa entered prison in 1967, but four years later President Richard Nixon commuted the sentence.

Banned from reentering Teamsters' politics until 1981, Hoffa was fighting the restriction in 1975 when he left his suburban home for a meeting with several union officials and several known members of the underworld. He arrived on time for the 2 P.M. meeting at a restaurant, but called his wife at 2:20 to say that no one else had showed up. He was then seen getting into a car in the restaurant parking lot at 2:45. And that was the last time anyone from the public saw Jimmy Hoffa.

Speculation has it that the underworld set up a hit, garroting Hoffa in the back of a car and destroying his body in a fat-rendering plant, to keep him from regaining his power.

The mobsters Hoffa was supposed to be meeting were rumored to have been involved in the murder, and authorities later found the car used in the abduction with Hoffa's blood and hair on the back seat. They have not been able to come up with enough evidence to prosecute anyone.

During Senate hearings into organized crime in 1988, FBI Director

William Sessions declared that the men the Bureau believed responsible for Hoffa's death were already in jail for other crimes.

Sessions also suggested a motive for Hoffa's disappearance: 'There was an expression, shortly before his death, that he intended to purge the organized crime families from the union's activities."

A year after the hearings, Hoffa's family demanded that the FBI divulge any information it had on the case. The Bureau refused, however, on grounds of confidentiality.

A former Mafia informant in a 1990 interview in *Playboy* magazine, claimed that Hoffa had been murdered, dismembered, and buried under Giants Stadium in East Rutherford, New Jersey. The FBI, however, said the story was unconfirmed and apparently no digging took place at the stadium.

The whereabouts of Jimmy Hoffa remain unknown.

Date: December 6, 1975
Site: Philadelphia, Pennsylvania
Type: Sex
Murderers: Salvatore Soli and Steven Maleno
Victim: John Knight III

••

JOHN KNIGHT III lived a classic double life. A working journalist, he was in fact heir to a newspaper publishing fortune. He collected fine art, dined in expensive restaurants, and lived in a luxurious apartment.

In that apartment, however, was a trunk that, when opened by the police, revealed another side of Knight's life. Inside were photographs of naked youths, sexual devices, and a sensational diary that shocked even some of Knight's closest friends. Police came across the trunk after finding Knight tied up and stabbed to death in his apartment.

Knight, thirty at the time of his death, was murdered early in the morning on December 6, 1975, after an evening that was described as typical in his life—dining out on pheasants he had shot himself on a hunting trip with a group of friends. After a leisurely dinner, Knight, a woman friend, and another couple returned to his apartment.

The woman soon left, but the couple stayed the night. At about 3 A.M. they awakened to a nightmarish sight. Knight had apparently let in three men, drifters in the area, who had tied him hand and foot, beat him severely, and then stabbed him in the chest and in the back.

The couple were harassed and threatened but lived to tell their tale.

The trunk that divulged Knight's secret was hard to open, but the key was finally located when a friend of Knight's came forward to give it up.

The friend said that Knight had often brought young boys to his apartment, but insisted that the evenings were "two percent sexual and ninety-eight percent fathering."

Many of Knight's other friends never caught on to the other side of his life, but authorities said that his sexual activities undoubtedly left him vulnerable to the type of attack that proved fatal.

Arrested soon after the murder were two men, Steven Maleno, twenty-five, and Salvatore Soli, thirty-seven, who were tried a year later and received life sentences for the murder. They were also suspected of murdering a third suspect in the case who had been found shot to death the same evening Knight was killed.

Date: February 12, 1976
Site: West Hollywood, California
Type: Robbery
Murderer: Lionel Ray Williams
Victim: Sal Mineo

MONEY AND SUCCESS are no guarantee of safety, and even in Hollywood not all stories end happily ever after.

Sal Mineo had appeared in over twenty feature films and dozens of television shows. Best known for his role in the 1955 James Dean movie, *Rebel Without a Cause,* he was nominated for an Academy Award as best supporting actor that year. Mineo was nominated in the same category again in 1960, this time for his role in *Exodus.* But Mineo made the biggest headlines on February 12, 1976.

At 10 P.M. that night, he parked his car in the carport beneath his West Hollywood apartment. Minutes later, neighbors heard the actor shout, "Oh no! Oh, my God, no! Help me, please!" One of the neighbors said that he ran outside and saw a man lying on his side in a fetal position. Turning the man over, he realized it was Mineo and that Mineo's entire chest was covered with blood.

Despite the neighbor's attempts to give mouth-to-mouth resuscitation, Mineo died on the spot. His heart had been pierced by a heavy-bladed knife. Car keys and untouched wallet remained at the actor's side.

Minutes after Mineo was stabbed, witnesses saw a man drive off in what appeared to be a yellow Toyota. The description of the car helped police track down the killer. But even more helpful was the suspect's own bragging.

First, Lionel Williams, twenty-one at the time, told his girlfriend, during a television news report of Mineo's murder, "That's the dude I killed." Whether she believed him or not, the girl did not immediately repeat his story to the police.

Coincidentally, however, Williams was later arrested and sent to Michigan to stand trial on a bad check charge. While in prison, Williams then told another inmate that he had killed someone, and when asked who by the cellmate, Williams had replied, "Sal Mineo."

Further investigation proved that the yellow Toyota seen leaving the crime was actually a similar-looking Dodge Colt that Williams had borrowed on the day of the murder.

And while the actual murder weapon was never found, more of Williams's bragging led the police to a store that sold a knife which could have made the wounds inflicted on Mineo. Williams had a tattoo depicting a similar knife on his arm.

A jury deliberated seven days and finally found Williams guilty of second-degree murder, along with ten counts of robbery. He was sentenced to fifty years in prison.

Date: May 4, 1976

Site: Elk Grove Village, Illinois

Type: Insurance fraud

Murderers: Patricia Columbo and Frank DeLuca

Victims: Frank, Mary, and Michael Columbo

....

THE FEROCITY OF the murder of Frank Columbo, forty-three, his forty-one-year-old wife, Mary, and their thirteen-year-old son, Michael, was shocking. Even more troubling however was the arrest days later of Frank and Mary's daughter, Patricia Columbo, and her thirty-nine-year-old lover, Frank DeLuca.

According to police the pair shot Frank in the head four times, his wife once. Both had been beaten and their throats were slashed. Michael was stabbed ninety-seven times. Among the murder weapons were a pair of scissors and a large trophy.

During the trial, several witnesses came forward to say that Patricia had offered men sexual favors if they would kill her family.

Prosecutors claimed that the killings were motivated by a feud between Frank Columbo and DeLuca, who had abandoned his wife and children to live with Patricia. Relatives also revealed that Patricia had hated her family for a long time.

The lovers were later found guilty of murder and sentenced to serve at least two hundred years in prison.

Date: July 1976

Site: Utah

Type: Robbery

Murderer: Gary Gilmore

Victims: Max Jensen and Bennie Bushnell

BRUTAL CRIMES are committed every day. What drew attention to the murders of twenty-four-year-old Max Jensen, a service station attendant, and twenty-five-year-old motel manager Bennie Bushnell was the punishment their killer, Gary Gilmore, received.

On January 17, 1977, less than a year after the murders, Gary Gilmore was shot by a firing squad at the Utah State Prison in Point of the Mountain, Utah. He was the first person to be executed in the United States in more than a decade.

The victims of robberies on consecutive nights, Jensen and Bushnell were killed the same way: Each man was told to lie down on the floor; each was shot in the head. The murderer, who said he was in a rage over the breakup of his relationship with his nineteen-year-old girlfriend, did not attempt to evade his punishment.

On the contrary, he told the judge who asked why he didn't file an appeal, "You sentenced me to die. Unless it's a joke or something, I want to go ahead and do it." Several groups attempted to file appeals on Gilmore's behalf, but he told one group to "butt out," and went on a twenty-five day hunger strike to foil the others.

Finally, after months of delays, Gilmore was strapped to a chair, and a target was placed over his heart. His last words were "Let's do it." Five men fired at Gilmore's heart. Four had bullets in their rifles; one had blanks (but no one knew who had the blanks). Gilmore died two minutes later.

Not only did the case attract worldwide attention from the press, but Norman Mailer wrote a best-selling book about it called *The Executioner's Song*. There was also a miniseries on television about Gilmore, starring Tommy Lee Jones.

Date: July 1976 to August 1977

Site: New York City

Type: Serial

Murderer: David Berkowitz

Victims: 6 people

....

HE IS PROBABLY less well known by his real name than by his nickname. But David Berkowitz's shooting spree made "Son of Sam" a name feared by millions.

In New York City between July 1976 and August 1977, Berkowitz murdered six people and wounded seven others with a .44-caliber handgun. Most of his victims were sitting in parked cars at the time of the attacks.

Under the signature "Son of Sam," the murderer had taunted police, sending letters to newspapers implicating himself in the crimes and gaining sensational media coverage.

On the night of what turned out to be the final murder in the string, Berkowitz walked up to a car in a Brooklyn parking lot at about 1:30 A.M. and shot its male and female occupants.

The woman, Stacy Moskowitz, a twenty-year-old blond, died less than four hours later of a bullet in her brain, thus becoming the killer's sixth victim. She had been lulled into a false sense of security because the killer—who was the subject of several public warnings from city officials—had previously targeted women with shoulder-length dark brown hair.

Immediately after the shooting, a man was spotted leaving the scene in a car that had just received a ticket for parking too near a fire hydrant.

A police check of all such tickets issued that evening led them to Berkowitz, a postal service worker living in an apartment in Yonkers. Neighbors later described him as someone who "acted crazy or goofy sometimes."

As he was led from his apartment by the police, Berkowitz greeted a detective assigned to the case: "Inspector Dowd! You finally got me!"

Berkowitz, who still had the murder weapon with him when arrested, was convicted and sentenced to three hundred and fifteen years in prison.

The case later received more attention when a proposed book telling Berkowitz's story was made the basis for a law to prevent criminals from reaping the benefits of royalties from books or movies about their crimes.

Date: 1977 to 1978

Site: Los Angeles County, California

Type: Sex

Murderers: Kenneth Bianchi and Angelo Buono

Victims: 12 females

••

THE MURDERERS were dubbed the "Hillside Stranglers" because of their way the female victims were found, usually raped and strangled, on hillsides in Los Angeles County.

The first two victims, it was reported, were prostitutes. But after that, the list included a waitress, a model, a fourteen-year-old, and a twelve-year-old, among others.

For four months in 1977 the murderers eluded the police, who had set up a special task force to investigate the deaths. But early in 1979 the police in Bellingham, Washington, found the bodies of two college students in a car belonging to one of them. The two students had been raped and murdered. The Bellingham police noted similarities to the widely publicized Hillside Strangler case and contacted the Los Angeles police. The L.A. police then went to Washington to question a suspect picked up in the case: twenty-seven-year-old Kenneth Bianchi.

Bianchi, who had moved to the Bellingham area from Los Angeles months earlier to live with his girlfriend and their child, denied any guilt. But he was held on a burglary charge after stolen goods were found in his home. A further search of one of the victims' rooms uncovered Bianchi's business card.

The suspect then claimed he was the victim of multiple personalities. To prove his point, the normally polite Bianchi gave psychiatric examiners a glimpse of a profane personality he called Steve, who was outspokenly contemptuous of all moral standards.

In a taped conversation with authorities, "Steve" described the murder of the Strangler's last victim, a woman who had come to Angelo Buono's car repair shop for floor mats for her car.

"Angelo was in the house talking to the girl. . . . I came in and grabbed her around the throat. . . . Nothing's said. . . . Angelo got up and went to get some rope, tied her, and gagged her."

"Steve" went on to tell how he and Buono had blindfolded the victim, made her remove her clothing, raped her, tied her hand and foot, then put a rope around her neck and strangled her.

There was a moment of silence on the tape and then Bianchi said, "What a cruel thing to do."

But Bianchi's multiple personality claim did not exonerate him, and he was charged with the multiple murders. He pleaded guilty to the two in Washington and five in California, and he received life sentences in both states.

Bianchi was eventually transferred to prison in Washington, where in 1989 he married a thirty-six-year-old woman he had begun corresponding with three years before.

Date: 1978 to 1991

Site: Milwaukee and West Allis, Wisconsin, and
   Conventry Township, Ohio

Type: Mass

Murderer: Jeffrey Dahmer

Victims: 17 Young boys and men

···

POLICE ON ROUTINE PATROL in the city of Milwaukee came across a man wearing handcuffs, frantically motioning to them as he ran down the street. They stopped and he directed them back to a nearby apartment where they discovered one of the most macabre murder scenes in U.S. history.

In the nondescript apartment building lived thirty-two-year-old Jeffrey Dahmer, himself a rather average-looking individual, though some described him as handsome.

But there was nothing average about Dahmer's apartment. It contained body parts from eleven murder victims, photographs of mutilated men, and painted human skulls.

Dahmer told the police that he had committed seventeen murders beginning in 1978 and ending just a few days before he was caught. His attorney later revealed that Dahmer had told him, "There comes a time you have to be honest."

Before he decided to come clean, however, Dahmer had lured his victims, many of them black homosexuals, to his apartment with promises of a party. Once there, they were drugged and killed.

One of the most shocking revelations came a few weeks after Dahmer's arrest, when it was discovered that police had visited his apartment at least once before to return a fourteen-year-old youth they had found walking naked in the nearby streets to his care.

When the neighbor who had called the police about the teenager called to ask what happened, an officer who responded told her it was just a "boyfriend-boyfriend thing"—a domestic situation between homosexuals. The officer, who had believed the youth was over eighteen, was shocked to learn that Dahmer had murdered him only hours after they'd brought him to the apartment.

The three officers involved were immediately suspended by the Milwaukee police chief, pending a full investigation.

Dahmer was described as strange by those who knew him in his youth.

Born in Ohio, he had moved to Milwaukee in 1981 after being discharged from the Army. A former high school classmate remembered, "He traced bodies on the floor in chalk."

Dahmer's Milwaukee murders apparently were preceded by a murder he had committed in Ohio and several others he committed at his grandmother's home in suburban West Allis.

Dahmer's victims ranged in age from their mid-teens to early thirties. Typically, he would have sex with them, then drug and kill them, dismembering their bodies and disposing of the bones. In some cases, he kept the skulls, which he spray painted gray to make them look like plastic. *The New York Times* reported that he "fried a victim's biceps in vegetable shortening and ate it," but the police would not confirm the story.

Although Dahmer's murders were apparently spread over a decade, he struck more frequently as he neared his arrest: His last three were committed on June 30, July 4, and July 19, 1991.

Dahmer pleaded guilty to the murders but claimed he was insane at the time. However, a jury found him sane in February of 1992, and he was sentenced to fifteen consecutive life terms in prison, with the earliest possible parole in about a thousand years.

The Milwaukee Journal

Jeffrey Dahmer

Date: November 27, 1978

Site: San Francisco, California

Type: Revenge

Murderer: Dan White

Victims: Mayor George Moscone and Harvey Milk

• •

ON JANUARY 6, 1984, a little more than five years after his conviction in the bold murders of the mayor of San Francisco and a city supervisor, thirty-two-year-old Dan White walked out of jail.

White, a former city supervisor himself had asked to be reappointed to his seat after resigning because the pay was not enough to support his family.

Mayor George Moscone had at first agreed to reappoint White, but then he changed his mind. Just before Moscone was to announce a replacement, White burst into the mayor's office and shot him four times.

White then went to the nearby office of Harvey Milk, a supervisor who had been against White's reinstatement, and shot him dead.

White was convicted only of manslaughter—not premeditated murder —in the deaths. Because Milk was known to be gay, the verdict provoked a violent reaction in San Francisco's homosexual community; more than 5,000 protesters accounted for over $1 million in damage to the city.

White's attorney used a controversial defense tactic, later dubbed the Twinkie Defense; claiming that White's consumption of junk food had affected his judgement. But the jury didn't buy it, and in 1979 White received the maximum sentence for manslaughter: seven years and eight months in prison. White was paroled in 1984.

In 1985, White committed suicide by attaching a garden hose to the exhaust pipe of his car and running the hose into the car. A note taped to the windshield read: "I knew you were going to find me this way. Sorry you had to find me in this condition. Sorry for any inconvenience."

One police officer said, "Those of us who knew him realized that this was going to happen sooner or later."

Dianne Feinstein, Moscone's successor as mayor, said, "I am very sorry to hear that Dan White has taken his life. My sympathy to his widow, Mary Ann, his children and his family, who have suffered very much. This latest tragedy should close a very sad chapter in this city's history."

But there were some in the gay community who called White's suicide "the perfect ending to a horrible story."

Date: April 28, 1979

Site: White Lick Creek, Indiana

Type: Sex

Murderer: Steven Judy

Victims: Terry Chasteen and her three children

··

WHEN STEVEN JUDY was twelve years old, he went to the door of a neighbor and asked if she wanted to buy Scout cookies. Once inside the house, he raped, stabbed, and almost hacked the woman to death. Judy was then sent to a mental institution, but for only nine months.

At eighteen, Judy spent twenty months in jail for badly beating a Chicago woman. A while after that, a young woman in Indianapolis barely escaped from his clutches; Judy spent another year in prison for car theft, kidnapping, and committing a felony while armed.

Then, on April 28, 1979, he pulled up alongside Terry Chasteen's car and motioned to her that there was something wrong with her tires.

When the woman, who was traveling with her three children, got out to check, Judy raised the hood of her car and pulled out the ignition coil. He then offered to drive her to a gas station. He drove instead to a secluded spot, told the woman's three children to take a walk, then forced the woman to undress, and raped her.

Chasteen's screams drew the children back. So Judy strangled her, and as the children returned, he picked them up one after another and drowned them in a nearby creek.

After he was found guilty of murder, Judy told the jury, "You had better put me to death, because the next time it might be one of you or your daughter."

Steven Judy fought all attempts to spare him from the electric chair. His wish to die was granted on March 8, 1981.

Date: October 1979 through May 1981

Site: Atlanta, Georgia

Type: Serial

Murderer: Wayne Williams

Victims: 24 to 28 men

....

THIS STRING of murders not only captured the public's attention; it became a matter of concern for then President Reagan and Vice President George Bush. Even Frank Sinatra got into the act.

Someone was murdering young black men in Atlanta, Georgia, while someone—or something else—was causing others to just disappear. Panic gripped the area, and black children were cautioned to avoid strangers.

Many of the victims' bodies were found naked. The men had been strangled or asphyxiated; most were found in rivers.

It was a baffling case, but simple police observation finally led to an arrest. On May 22, 1981, police on a stakeout at a bridge across the Chattahoochee River heard a splash and then saw a man get into a car. They stopped the individual, twenty-three-year-old Wayne Williams. He claimed he had thrown garbage into the river.

Williams, a local music promoter and TV cameraman, was released. But days later, when the body of another victim was found in the river, the case against Williams began to mount.

A month later, Williams was charged with several of the murders. Dog hair, found on several of the victims' bodies, were also found in Williams's home. Moreover, investigators learned that Williams had been seen with some of the victims before they died.

Tried on two counts of murder, in the cases of a twenty-one-year-old and a twenty-seven-year-old, Williams was found guilty and sentenced to two life terms.

Though some people charged that Williams had been made a scapegoat in the case, possibly to cover up for another murderer, no similar murders have occurred since his imprisonment.

Date: March 10, 1980

Site: Purchase, New York

Type: Jealousy

Murderer: Jean Harris

Victim: Dr. Herman Tarnower

JEAN HARRIS was as unlikely a murderer as one could imagine. A woman with sophistication, elegance, and charm, she had graduated from a prestigious prep school and received an economics degree from Smith College. At the time of the crime, she was headmistress of a girls' boarding school in Virginia called the Madeira School.

After a failed marriage, Harris had met Dr. Herman Tarnower, a confirmed bachelor, in the mid-1960s. The two began a passionate relationship that would last more than a decade.

By 1980, Harris and Tarnower were still together, but things were clearly changing. Tarnower, at sixty-nine, had become an instant celebrity when his book, *The Complete Scarsdale Medical Diet* zoomed to the top of the best-seller list. More to the point, Harris now had a rival in Lynne Tryforos, thirty-eight, who had been an employee of Tarnower's medical clinic.

Tarnower was not secretive about his relationship with his new and younger mistress. He would leave evidence of the other woman's presence, including her nightwear, where he knew Harris would see it. Harris, who was still in love with Tarnower, begged him to stop seeing Tryforos, but the doctor refused.

By February 1980, Harris had fallen into what some described as a suicidal depression. She purchased a .32-caliber revolver and, on the evening of March 10, wrote a series of letters, including a resignation from her position at Madeira, a will, and instructions for her funeral.

According to Harris's later testimony, she then drove from the school in Virginia to Tarnower's swanky home in Purchase, New York. She intended to say good-bye to him and then commit suicide. But when she arrived at 10:30 P.M., Harris found Tryforos's nightgown and hair curlers in Tarnower's bathroom.

After throwing the curlers out the window, Harris confronted Tarnower in his bedroom. She then took out her .32-caliber revolver and tried to shoot herself. But somehow, Harris insisted, she accidentally shot Tarnower when he tried to grab the weapon away from her.

A housekeeper heard the noise and called the police. When they found him, Tarnower had been shot four times, once in the back. The police also caught Harris attempting to leave the residence, but she claimed she was only going for help.

Jean Harris was charged with second-degree murder. (In New York State, first-degree murder is reserved strictly for the killing of law enforcement officers and prison guards.)

But while the defense claimed that Harris shot Tarnower accidentally during the struggle for her gun, witnesses at the trial gave damaging evidence to the contrary. One police officer testified that shortly after the shooting, Harris said, "He slept with every woman he could. I had to do it."

The housekeeper claimed that Harris had told Tarnower and his younger lover she would "make their lives miserable."

And a deputy medical examiner said that Tarnower's four wounds, including the one in the back, were hardly "consistent with a struggle over a gun."

The jury spent eight days deliberating and ended up finding Harris guilty. While Harris showed no reaction to the verdict, two defense lawyers burst into tears when it was announced.

Members of the jury later explained that when they tried to re-enact the murder scene, Harris's story seemed unconvincing. "We acted it out so many times," said one juror. "We went through the motions in the bedroom, and it didn't turn out the way Mrs. Harris said it did."

Harris was given the minimum sentence of fifteen years to life, with parole possible in 1996.

There have since been numerous attempts to win clemency for her. In 1986, nationally syndicated columnist James J. Kilpatrick asked that her plea for clemency to New York Governor Mario Cuomo be heard. "Harris was sixty-three years old in April," he wrote at the time. "She has suffered two serious heart attacks in prison. Governor Cuomo and his advisers might well ask themselves what possible public purpose is served by keeping her longer in prison."

But Cuomo rejected that and subsequent requests. After exhausting possible appeals on the state level, Harris has moved her case to federal court. She is in prison in Bedford Hills, New York.

Date: June 6, 1980

Site: Libertyville, Illinois

Type: Unknown

Murderer: Unknown

Victims: Bruce and Darlene Rouse

••

OFFICIALLY, THE MURDERS of Bruce and Darlene Rouse are listed as unsolved. But authorities, accused of bungling the case hours after the crime was committed, may in fact know the killer yet be unable to prove it in court.

The Rouses were brutally murdered in a bedroom of their expensive home near Libertyville, Illinois, a suburb of Chicago on June 6, 1980.

Authorities think Darlene Rouse, thirty-eight, was killed first when the murderer pressed a shotgun between her eyes and pulled the trigger, killing her instantly. The blast probably awakened Bruce Rouse, forty-four, who was met with another gun blast which severely damaged his face but did not kill him. The murderer then beat Rouse about the head with the gun butt and stabbed him several times in the heart.

Despite the fact that the three Rouse children were all sleeping in the house or elsewhere on the property, the bodies were not discovered until the next morning when an employee at one of the several service stations Bruce Rouse owned called to find out the combination for a safe.

Only then did sixteen-year-old Robin Rouse find her parents' bodies. She summoned her brother, Billy, who was fifteen at the time, and he called the police.

When police arrived they also found the Rouse's other son, twenty-year-old Kurt. Robin, they noted was distraught, but the two boys seemed relatively composed.

Robin and Billy, who had been sleeping in bedrooms one floor above their parents' room, both said they had heard nothing—as did Kurt, who had spent the night in a small cottage behind the main house.

Authorities found nothing missing from the Rouses' home—except for all their guns. Cash and jewelry were untouched. The murder weapon was later found in a nearby river, wiped clean of fingerprints.

The police attempted to question the Rouse children—who stood to inherit millions from their parents' estate—but they had hired attorneys who advised them not to speak. Later, the young Rouses invoked their Fifth Amendment right not to incriminate themselves.

Digging into the family's past, police found that Kurt was at the center of some family problems. The Rouses had tried to get him to join the Army, but after promising to do so, he'd changed his mind.

Police suspect that the Rouse children knew what had happened. Their best chance, they felt, was to get Robin Rouse talking. But she was killed in a traffic accident in August 1983.

One official close to the investigation said that the police had made a huge mistake when they failed to separate the children immediately to get individual stories.

No arrest has yet been made in the case.

Date: August 15, 1980
Site: Los Angeles, California
Type: Revenge
Murderer: Paul Snider
Victim: Dorothy Stratten

....

DOROTHY STRATTEN was truly lovely. She had appeared in *Playboy* as the August 1979 centerfold, and, at the age of twenty, was named the magazine's Playmate of the Year. An aspiring actress, she had appeared in several films and was romantically involved with movie director Peter Bogdanovich.

But Dorothy Stratten's past life caught up with her in August 1980, in the form of her estranged husband, Paul Snider. Snider had "discovered" Stratten in her hometown of Vancouver, British Columbia. He romanced her, then sent nude pictures of her to *Playboy.*

Hugh Hefner, the publisher of *Playboy,* was so impressed with the photos that he flew Stratten to Hollywood and put her up in his mansion. Hefner also introduced her to Bogdanovich. The director cast Stratten in a movie, and the two eventually fell in love.

As soon as she returned to Hollywood from shooting the movie in New York, Stratten told Snider she wanted a divorce and refused to live with him.

On August 15, 1980, a despondent Snider went to Stratten's home. Friends later found Stratten sprawled across the bed. She had been killed by a shotgun blast to the face. Snider was also found dead, of a self-inflicted shotgun blast.

In 1984, Bogdanovich wrote a book, *The Killing of the Unicorn: Dorothy Stratten, 1960-1980,* in which he attempted to place some of the blame for Stratten's death on Hefner. Weeks after it was published, Hefner said that he had suffered a mild stroke as a result of "stress developed over the last year in reaction to the pathological book written by Peter Bogdanovich."

Bogdanovich replied that he was sorry about Hefner's illness, but then added, "Confronting Hugh Hefner with the reality of his life, and in particular what he and his magazine do to women, apparently is something he can't face."

Bogdanovich later married Stratten's younger sister, Louise.

Date: December 5, 1980

Site: Washington, D.C.

Type: Robbery

Murderer: Bernard Welch

Victim: Dr. Michael Halberstam

••

BERNARD WELCH was considered a master burglar. Federal authorities found him almost impossible to catch, and once caught, even more difficult to hold.

It has been estimated that during his criminal career, Welch netted between $10 and $20 million. His home in Virginia, raided after his arrest, was filled with rare works of art as well as coins, furs, and jewelry.

One of the keys to Welch's success was the fact that he was smart enough to refrain from violence unless he was threatened. But that is exactly what happened on the evening of December 5, 1980, when Welch was attempting to burglarize the home of Dr. Michael Halberstam, a prominent physician, whose brother, David, won a Pulitzer Prize for his book on the Kennedy Administration.

Welch was caught in the act by Halberstam and his wife as they returned home. The two men tangled, and then Welch fired twice, hitting Halberstam in the chest, and ran.

The physician was able to drive himself to the hospital, however, and on the way there he spotted Welch. Halberstam swerved the car to hit him, leaving the burglar sprawled on the sidewalk for authorities to arrest.

Halberstam died on the operating table a short time later. Welch was convicted of murder and sentenced to nine consecutive life terms.

Date: December 8, 1980

Site: New York City

Type: Assassination

Murderer: Mark David Chapman

Victim: John Lennon

••

MARK DAVID CHAPMAN was a big fan of John Lennon—until a picture in a book changed his attitude.

"I was looking for a way to vent all the disappointment, my anger, my rage," Chapman was to say ten years after he killed Lennon. Chapman, who considered himself "a complete failure," went on to explain his lethal change of heart: "I opened the book and I saw him—put yourself where I was—I saw him on the roof of the gabled, luxurious Dakota apartment [building]. And I became hurt, enraged at what I perceived to be his phoniness."

Chapman, decided he would have to kill Lennon.

Chapman was then living in Hawaii, and Lennon in new York City. But that didn't stop the would-be assassin. Selling a valuable lithograph and signing out from his job as a security guard as "John Lennon," Chapman flew to New York. But when he arrived he was unable to buy bullets for his .38-caliber revolver or to gain access to Lennon. And so he flew back to Hawaii in November of 1980.

A month later, Chapman returned to New York City. In the late afternoon of December 8, 1980, he waited outside Lennon's apartment building on New York's Upper West Side, holding up a copy of Lennon's latest album. When Lennon and his wife, Yoko Ono, finally appeared, Lennon stopped and autographed it.

Still, Chapman lingered. Questioned by the doorman, he said he wanted to get Ono's autograph as well.

When Lennon and Ono returned at about 11 P.M., Chapman was waiting for them at the entrance to the Dakota. This time he called out, "Mr. Lennon," and as Lennon started to turn, Chapman put five bullets into his back.

Lennon fell to the ground. One of the doormen on duty ripped off his tie to use as a tourniquet to staunch the bleeding. But there was no way to control the blood streaming from Lennon's chest and mouth.

By the time the police arrived, it was clear that Lennon could not wait for the ambulance, so they put him in the back of a squad car and sped to

Roosevelt Hospital. Despite their efforts, Lennon was declared dead on arrival.

At first the police thought the doorman who had tried to help Lennon was the killer, since he was covered with blood and appeared wild-eyed. But another doorman on duty pointed to a young man who stood calmly on the street, reading *The Catcher in the Rye.*

Chapman pleaded guilty to the murder and insisted that he was sane. He was sentenced to a term of twenty years to life in prison. He will not be eligible for parole until the year 2000.

On the ten-year anniversary of the murder, Chapman was quoted extensively. When he asked the world to forgive him: "You can't judge a man's life by one act. Before I became the man who murdered John Lennon, I was basically a decent person," he told the Rochester (New York) *Democrat and Chronicle.*

"When Lennon's limousine pulled up, he got out and he looked at me," Chapman went on. "I'm sure he remembered me. I walked back into the driveway and took the combat stance, just the way I'd practiced in my hotel room.

"It was an end of innocence for that time. And I regret being the one that ended it."

Date: January 6, 1981

Site: Idaho

Type: Cop killing

Murderer: Claude Dallas, Jr.

Victims: Bill Pogue and Conley Elms

Claude Dallas, Jr.

GUNFIGHTERS OF THE Wild West—many of them murderers—have long been romanticized as heroes in movies and novels. But in real life, murder is another story.

In 1981, Claude Dallas, Jr., a self-styled mountain man, killed two game wardens who came upon his campsite and tried to arrest him for poaching. The wardens had gone to check on reports that someone was hunting deer and trapping bobcats out of season.

It took law enforcement authorities more than a year to track and capture Dallas, in part because he had been receiving help from his neighbors, who left pickup trucks with gas in the tanks and food on the seats for his use.

When Dallas was finally tried, a jury found him guilty only on two counts of voluntary manslaughter instead of the first-degree murder he'd been charged with.

During the trial Dallas had claimed he shot the wardens in self-defense. According to Dallas, Pogue drew his gun first.

The jury foreman said that the jurors, who deliberated more than a week, "figured Pogue drew his gun, and Dallas was a better marksman. Dallas was faster on the draw. He won out."

But the juror also said that Dallas had gone beyond self-defense after shooting the two men when he then fired one bullet into each officer's head with a .22-caliber rifle.

Dallas was sentenced to thirty years in prison. But the story of Claude Dallas, Jr., did not end there.

On March 30, 1986, Dallas escaped from jail by cutting through two heavy-gauge chainlink fences. The escape hardly surprised those who knew him. "Everybody said they knew he was going to escape," said the prison warden. "Even his lawyer, when we told him, said, 'I kinda figured on that.' "

Although the FBI put Dallas on its Ten Most Wanted list, he evaded authorities for over a year, but he was finally arrested peacefully on March 8, 1987, at a convenience store in Riverside, California.

Date: May 28, 1981

Site: Milwaukee, Wisconsin

Type: Unknown

Murderer: Lawrencia Bembenek

Victim: Christine Schultz

··

THE BUMPER STICKERS and shirts read "Run, Bambi, Run" but they weren't referring to the famous fawn. Instead, they were urging a convicted murderess, who had escaped from a Wisconsin prison, to keep free of the law.

As implausible as it seems, many people in the state of Wisconsin were hoping that "Bambi"—the nickname for Lawrencia Bembenek—would be able to get away with what many others were convinced was murder.

Bembenek's fate had become a cause célèbre in the years following her conviction for the murder of her then husband's ex-wife, Christine Schultz.

Why had she captivated so many people?

For starters, Bembenek was beautiful. A former *Playboy* bunny, she had posed for brewery calendars in skimpy outfits, though, as one fan put it, she would have looked good even in a potato sack.

Not long after her conviction, the tide of public opinion turned to skepticism over Bembenek's guilt. And while local concern for her continued years after she was first jailed in Wisconsin, her reputation became truly international when she escaped from prison in July 1990.

She was captured three months later in Thunder Bay, Ontario, where she was working as a waitress and living with her lover, Dominic Gugliatto, a Milwaukee factory worker who had met and fallen in love with Bambi while she was in prison.

Bembenek's conviction for the murder of Christine Schultz had been based largely on circumstantial evidence. In the early morning hours of May 28, 1981, someone dressed in a green jogging suit had broken into Schultz's home and gagged and bound the thirty-one-year-old mother of two. After attempting to tie up one of the two young boys in the house, the intruder had gone back to Christine's room and shot her in the heart once with a .38-caliber revolver.

On June 24, 1981, Bembenek, who five months earlier had married Elfred Schultz, a detective with the Milwaukee Police Department, was charged with the murder.

Among the evidence presented at the trial was a reddish-brown wig,

142

found in an apartment next-door to the one in which Schultz and Bembenek lived; there was also a black and white photo of Bembenek wearing what appeared to be a green jogging suit. But the biggest blow to the defense came when Bambi was quoted as saying she knew the right people to have Christine Schultz "blown away."

Lawrencia Bembenek was found guilty in March 1982 and sentenced to life in prison.

Appeals began almost immediately, and several private investigators and suitors took up her cause. Fingers were pointed at Elfred Schultz, and he and Bembenek were divorced in 1984. The two spent the next few years accusing each other of the murder.

Three appeals were launched on Bembenek's behalf; all three failed. Finally, in 1990, Bambi, then thirty-two, escaped from prison. But within months she was back in custody. Canadian officials arrested her after receiving a tip from someone who saw her story on "America's Most Wanted" television show.

Bembenek fought deportation for a while, seeking refugee status, claiming she had not had a fair trial in the United States and was being unfairly persecuted. Then, early in 1992, she abandoned the fight against extradition. She is still in prison in Canada but will soon be returned to the United States.

Date: July 10, 1981

Site: Skidmore, Missouri

Type: Vigilantism

Murderer: Unknown

Victim: Ken Rex McElroy

....

FEW PEOPLE MOURN when a neighborhood bully gets beat up. Ken Rex McElroy, however, was a bigger-than-average bully. So it was hardly surprising that few people mourned when he got killed.

And when Ken Rex McElroy was shot to death in front of sixty people in broad daylight, not one of them could say who had killed him. Townsfolk were soon wearing T-shirts that read: "Who Killed K.R.?" on the front—and "Who gives a damn?" on the back.

For McElroy had all but held the town of Skidmore, Missouri, hostage for years. He once threatened a county deputy sheriff with a shotgun and knife. At the trial, no witnesses would testify and so he went free. There were other trials, one for attempted murder. But witnesses to the crimes would always claim they had seen nothing—if, that is, they dared to show up at all.

A well-known womanizer, McElroy had four wives and at least eleven children. He also had money by the bagful.

At five-foot-ten, and 265 pounds, McElroy was not abnormally big. But he had massive arms, a piercing gaze, and he carried guns and knives which he not only brandished threateningly but sometimes used.

The incident that finally provoked McElroy's murder was the wounding of a shopkeeper named Ernest "Bo" Bowenkamp. Bowenkamp had made the mistake of telling McElroy's daughter to put a piece of candy back if she wasn't going to pay for it.

After that, McElroy began haunting Bo, driving slowly past the man's home in his pickup truck. After a while of this, McElroy confronted Bo, who was much older, and challenged him to a fight. When Bo refused, McElroy fired at him with a shotgun, hitting his left shoulder and neck.

For once, McElroy was not able to win in court. But even after he was found guilty in the shooting of Bowenkamp, he was set free pending legal hearings. Some folks feared that McElroy might get away.

He didn't.

On July 10, 1981, McElroy had a beer at the D&G tavern. Afterward, a crowd followed him outside and watched as he got into the driver's side of his truck. His wife Trena climbed in beside him.

As McElroy put the keys into the ignition, a volley of shots rang out. Two or three hit him in the head, neck, and back. Finally Trena called for an ambulance, but McElroy was already dead.

Despite a coroner's inquest, and investigations by federal and state officials, no criminal charges were ever filed in the case. Some sixty people witnessed the shooting, and yet no one saw a thing.

Date: July 18, 1981

Site: New York City

Type: Celebrity

Murderer: Jack Henry Abbott

Victim: Richard Adan

··

IT SOUNDS LIKE a novel plot: A famous writer befriends a jailed criminal whose writing from the cell becomes a national best-seller.

The story, however, was true. But it didn't end happily ever after.

It all began with Jack Henry Abbott, who was first sentenced to prison when he was twelve years old. Abbott had managed to spend most of his life in jail for crimes ranging from bank robbery to murder.

During his imprisonment, Abbott started corresponding with author Norman Mailer, who was impressed with the convict's writing. Mailer helped Abbott publish his letters in a book, *In the Belly of the Beast,* which *The New York Times* called "a work touched with dark greatness." It became a best-seller.

Eventually, Mailer took part in an effort to obtain Abbott's release, writing letters pointing to his talent as a writer and even offering to give Abbott a job. Others in the publishing community wrote similar letters.

On June 5, 1981, Abbott was sent to a halfway house in New York City, prior to a full parole set for August 25 of the same year. But only a month later he went to a restaurant where he argued with a waiter, whom he asked to step outside. There Abbott killed twenty-two-year-old Richard Adan, an actor and playwright, with a knife. Then he fled.

When Abbott was caught and tried in 1982, a jury found him guilty of first-degree manslaughter instead of murder, claiming he had been so scarred by confinement that he could not be judged like a normal man. Abbott, who had spent all but ten months since the age of fourteen in police custody, seemed fundamentally incapable of living lawfully in the world outside prison. He was sentenced to fifteen years in prison for the crime.

In 1990, Abbott lost again, this time a civil case brought by his victim's widow. During the trial, Abbott, who acted as his own lawyer, scoffed at the courtroom tears of Ricci Adan; he then claimed she had prejudiced the jury against him and asked for a mistrial. The judge disagreed, and the jury eventually awarded Mrs. Adan $7.6 million in financial damages, with the money to come from proceeds of the books and movie scripts written by Abbott while in prison.

Date: July 27, 1981
Site: Hollywood, Florida
Type: Child
Murderer: Unknown
Victim: Adam Walsh

•••

EVEN THOUGH THE murderer of eight-year-old Adam Walsh has never been identified, it can be said that some good came from that monstrous crime.

Young Adam disappeared from outside a department store on July 27, 1981. Two weeks later, his severed head was discovered floating in a canal near Vero Beach, Florida, just hours after his parents made a nationally televised appeal for help in finding their son. The rest of his body was never found.

A little over two years after Adam Walsh's death, a television show recounting the tragic story was followed by the pictures of other missing children. Within hours dozens of phone calls helped authorities solve a number of disappearances—but not Adam's.

And after Adam's parents, John and Reve Walsh, began a national campaign, Congress passed the Missing Children's Act, which enlisted the aid of the FBI's computer network to help authorities in their search for youngsters who have disappeared.

Adam's murder seemed to be solved in late 1983 when Ottis Toole, who along with Henry Lucas (see page 148) was responsible for more than 500 murders, told detectives that he had killed the boy. According to the police, his statements included details that only the killer could have known.

Toole led the police to the site where he said he'd buried the youngster's body, but they found nothing. Later, Toole denied the murder; he and Lucas both recanted almost all of the murders they had taken credit for.

In 1991, Adam's murder was briefly thought to be the work of another suspected serial killer, when Jeffrey Dahmer of Milwaukee, Wisconsin, was arrested for the deaths of at least seventeen youths in Wisconsin and Ohio (see page 128). Learning that Dahmer had spent some time in Florida, the police there said they would look into the possibility that he was responsible. Dahmer, however, was never charged with the crime—nor, to this day, was anyone else.

Date: August 23, 1982

Site: Stoneburg, Texas

Type: Serial

Murderers: Henry Lee Lucas and Ottis Elwood Toole

Victims: Unknown—possibly 600

··

THE STORY OF Henry Lee Lucas and Ottis Elwood Toole is truly unbelievable—though at various times the authorities were convinced that they spoke the truth.

Lucas—who was accompanied at times by Ottis Elwood Toole—may have been the most prolific murderer in U.S. history. Or he may only have killed his mother.

In any event, Lucas confessed to more than 600 murders, apparently solving more than 200 cases in twenty-six states with his admissions.

But in 1985, as Lucas awaited the death penalty for one of those murders, the Dallas *Times Herald* reported that he may instead have been the perpetrator of the largest hoax in law-enforcement annals. The newspaper story claimed that he might have been guilty of three murders and that police had accepted his confessions to the others without sufficient supporting evidence.

In the frenzy that followed Lucas's arrest in June 1982, dozens of law enforcement officials from all over the country had linked Lucas and Toole to various murders in their states by eliciting what they considered key information from Lucas. In many cases they followed up with charges.

As it turned out, the one murder Lucas did not recant was the 1960 stabbing of his mother, for which he was sentenced to twenty to forty years in prison. Paroled in 1970, Lucas was arrested a year later and again imprisoned, this time for four years, for attempting to kidnap two teenage girls.

Lucas's next arrest came in 1982, in connection with the disappearance of his teenage wife, Becky, and an elderly woman for whom he had once worked.

In 1985, Lucas was sentenced to die in Texas for the death of an unidentified female hitchhiker. But after the *Times Herald* story appeared, he announced that the only person he had killed was his mother and that he had confessed to the other hundreds of slayings just because Texas Rangers had encouraged him to do so.

According to Lucas, the Texas Rangers and "other police departments

. . . with cases they wanted cleared," had led him to numerous crime scenes, told him how the crimes were committed, and showed him photographs to help with his confessions. By 1990, with execution set for December 1990, a fifty-four-year-old Lucas who spent his days in prison making pillowcases and wooden clocks, was still insisting that he had killed no one except his mother, and that he had killed her by accident.

The execution was stayed only hours before it was scheduled to be carried out.

Toole meanwhile was found guilty of setting a fire in a Jacksonville, Florida, boarding house that killed one man. Although he was sentenced to death in the electric chair, his sentence was voided by the Florida Supreme Court, which ordered a new sentencing hearing. This time the prosecution did not seek a new death sentence, and Toole was ordered to serve a life term with no chance of parole for twenty-five years.

Date: September 29 and 30, 1982

Site: Chicago

Type: Poisoning

Murderer: Unknown

Victims: Mary Kellerman; Theresa, Stanley, and
Adam Janus; Mary Reiner; Mary McFarland;
Paula Prince.

··

THE 1982 TYLENOL POISONINGS in the Chicago area had the entire nation
terrified of a drug that was usually considered benign and efficacious.
Any unsolved murder is perplexing. But this random mass murder seems
inexplicable.

Someone had been tampering with capsules of Extra-Strength Tylenol,
made by Johnson & Johnson, and the results were deadly:

• On September 29, 1982, Mary Kellerman, a twelve-year-old garde-
school student, took two capsules in the morning, became sick, and
died within hours.
• On the same day, in Arlington Heights, Illinois, twenty-seven-year-
old Adam Janus took two capsules, and then he too died within hours.
• Another twenty-seven-year-old, Mary Reiner, who had recently
given birth to a child was rushed to a local hospital after taking two
capsules and died there before a diagnosis could be made.
• A thirty-one-year-old woman, Mary McFarland, took two capsules,
and also died, despite being hospitalized.
• Relatives who arrived at the Janus house, to help make funeral ar-
rangements for Adam—his twenty-five-year-old brother, Stanley, and
Stanley's nineteen-year-old wife, Theresa—took Tylenol before the
danger was discovered. They both died.
• That same day, thirty-five-year-old Paula Jean Prince, a flight attendant, stopped at a drugstore, picked up some Tylenol, and died alone
in her apartment.

These deaths seemed unconnected until a reporter who was studying
the coroners' reports pointed out the victims' Tylenol use.

Immediately, the public was warned to refrain from taking Tylenol.
Early tests showed that the capsules had been opened and the Tylenol
compound removed and then replaced with deadly cyanide.

Although all the tainted capsules had come from one manufacturing lot, samples from that same lot at Johnson & Johnson's Pennsylvania factory were tested and found pure. The tampering most likely had occurred after the product reached drugstore shelves. To make matters worse, other "copy-cat" poisonings were soon being reported throughout the nation.

Within days, a task force of local and federal investigators, including the FBI, was assembled to work on the case.

While more than 2,000 suspects were eventually investigated, and more than 20,000 pages of data were compiled, only one individual drew the authorities' attention: Richard Lewis, who sent a letter to Johnson & Johnson's McNeil Laboratories demanding that they pay him $1 million to stop the killing.

Lewis had been indicted in 1978 on a murder charge, but was freed because of legal technicalities. In 1982 he was investigated for credit-card fraud while living in Kansas City. After being fired from his job in Chicago, he moved to New York—in September of 1982, the month of the murders.

Once apprehended, Lewis, thirty-five at the time, admitted to writing the letter but denied the actual poisonings. He was tried and sentenced to ten years for extortion.

To this day, the case remains open, despite a $100,000 reward offered by Johnson & Johnson.

As a result of this case, strong laws were enacted to prevent the possibility of similar tampering. Drug containers (and the packages for many other products) are now safety-sealed in a variety of ways.

Date: February 13, 1983

Site: Heaton, North Dakota

Type: Escape

Murderer: Gordon Kahl

Victims: Kenneth Muir, Robert Cheshire, Gene Matthews

....

GORDON KAHL was a member of Posse Comitatus, a paramilitary survivalist group that claimed to be a champion of law and order. But on February 13, 1983, Kahl refused to allow law enforcement authorities to arrest him, and in the ensuing shootout he killed two federal marshals.

Kahl had been convicted of evading federal income taxes. Like many Posse members, he refused to pay taxes for political reasons. As a condition of his probation, he was supposed to check in with a federal probation officer in Bismarck, North Dakota.

But when Kahl did not show up, and when federal agents learned he was planning to attend a tax protest meeting on February 13, they set out to arrest him.

According to witnesses, Kahl shouted, "I'm not going to let them take me again!" and then began firing a machine gun at the agents, hitting and killing U.S. marshals Kenneth Muir and Robert Cheshire. Other agents returned his fire, but Kahl escaped unharmed.

An intense manhunt that included armored vehicles was organized to track Kahl down. Four months went by without a clue. Then finally a resident of Little Rock, Arkansas, saw Kahl's picture on an FBI poster and reported that he had seen the suspect with a local couple.

Police and FBI agents staked out the couple's home. Outside, they found Leonard Ginter, who then called his wife out before telling the authorities that Kahl was inside.

When officers entered the house, Kahl shot and hit one. The police retreated, then fired tear gas, which caught on fire and exploded.

Apparently the place had been filled with dynamite and thousands of rounds of ammunition. Kahl's body was burned so badly that identification could not at first be made. The officer shot in the incident, Gene Matthews, also died.

Because Kahl had been a World War II veteran, his family wanted a funeral with full military honors, but the Air Force refused. Meanwhile, about seven hundred people, including two-hundred-and-fifty law enforcement officers, crowded into a small church in Walnut Ridge, Arkansas, for the funeral of Officer Matthews.

Date: July 7, 1983
Site: Los Angeles, California
Type: Celebrity
Murderer: Marvin Pancoast
Victim: Vicki Morgan

VICKI MORGAN was the mistress of multimillionaire Alfred Bloomingdale. Although he was many years older than she, Morgan found him fascinating. He was the heir to his family's department store fortune and a member of then President Ronald Reagan's "kitchen cabinet."

But their twelve-year affair ended bitterly. Morgan filed several lawsuits against Bloomingdale, including a $10 million palimony suit, claiming that she had been his companion, confidante, and sexual therapist. A judge had dismissed most of one suit describing Morgan as a well-paid prostitute.

Morgan, however, was never able to follow through on the final suit. For July 7, 1983, Marvin Pancoast walked into a police station and announced that he had killed her.

Despite receiving monthly payments of $10,000 to $18,000 from Bloomingdale during their relationship, Morgan was apparently nearly broke at the time of her death. Pancoast, who had met Morgan in 1979 at a clinic where both were being treated for depression, later explained that it was a stream of complaints about her finances that drove him to strike her repeatedly with a baseball bat. According to Pancoast, who said he was gay, the two had not been lovers.

In a confession he later repudiated, Pancoast said "I didn't want to kill her. I just wanted to go to sleep. I wanted her to be quiet for a while. I was tired.

"God acts in many strange ways. Maybe He had me do it. If so, I can dig my own grave, too."

Pancoast also said that on the night of the murder, he had attempted to help Morgan fall asleep by rubbing her feet with baby oil after two bottles of wine and an unspecified number of tranquilizers had failed to do the job.

"I fell asleep awhile and then woke up all sweaty and nervous and scared," Pancoast said. "She was awake and smoking.

"I started upstairs, and I remembered that baseball bat lying there in the dining room. The first time I hit her she raised up. She didn't say anything. I kept hitting her."

At his trial, Pancoast pleaded not guilty by reason of insanity. But a jury found him both guilty and sane. Pancoast was sentenced to twenty-six years to life in late 1984.

But perhaps the most sensational revelation came before the trial when one of Pancoast's first defense attorneys claimed he knew of the existence of video tapes that included footage of "sadomasochistic sex parties" involving Morgan, Bloomingdale, a congressman, and four Reagan administration appointees and friends.

The tapes, the attorney suggested, might have had something to do with Morgan's murder. The tapes, however, were never brought forward; the attorney said they had been stolen from his office.

In 1985, a defense attorney said that a jailed Pancoast had AIDS.

He died in 1991 in prison of an AIDS-related disease at the age of 42.

Date: October 5, 1983

Site: Seattle, Washington

Type: Mass

Murderers: Wai-Chu Ng, Kwan Mak, Benjamin Ng

Victims: 13 People

··

SEATTLE POLICE had apparently known for years about the Wah-My Club, a private Chinese social club that was often the scene of high-stakes gambling. But the entire nation learned about it in October 1983, when thirteen people, mostly elderly Asian men, were massacred execution-style in an apparent robbery.

According to police, "The bodies were just strewn around the floor." Most of the victims had been bound and then shot in the head with a .22-caliber gun.

The authorities were alerted when a lone survivor, shot in the neck, was seen staggering into the street.

A man who had frequented the club before the murders said that many of the people killed were dealers and bankers. They may have had up to $50,000 in cash among them.

Benjamin Ng, twenty, and Kwan Mak, twenty-two, both natives of Hong Kong, were arrested shortly after the murders. A third suspect, Wai-Chu Ng (no relation to Benjamin Ng) became the object of an intense manhunt, and on June 15, 1984, was named to the FBI's Ten Most Wanted list. He was arrested four months later, in the Chinatown section of Calgary, in Alberta, Canada, by the Royal Canadian Mounted Police.

Mak received a death sentence for the crimes; Benjamin Ng, life imprisonment without parole; and Wai-Chu Ng, thirteen life terms.

FBI

Wai-Chu Ng

Date: February through April 1984

Site: Florida, Texas, Oklahoma, Colorado, Nevada, New York

Type: Serial

Murderer: Christopher Wilder

Victims: 8 women

....

CHRISTOPHER WILDER was an unlikely mass murderer. Handsome and seemingly well off, with a charming Australian accent, he was also an accomplished auto racer.

Wilder, however, was not the man he seemed. Having had left Australia under suspicion in the kidnapping of two young girls, he was already in therapy and on probation in the United States after an arrest in a case involving sex with a young girl. He was also a prime suspect in the disappearance of two attractive women in Florida.

In 1984, Wilder went on a five-week cross-country spree of rape and murder. By the time it was over, twelve women had been abducted. Eight of them were either found dead or never found at all.

Wilder posed as a fashion photographer, convincing several women that he could help them win professional modeling contracts if they would come to his studio and let him photograph them. Most of the women were never seen alive again.

Wilder's first victim was Rosaria Gonzales, twenty, a part-time model who disappeared while she was handing out cigarette samples at the Miami Grand Prix.

It was that case, and the disappearance of Elizabeth Ann Kenyon, that prompted police and private investigators hired by the missing women's families, to consider Wilder as a suspect.

With the police moving in, Wilder checked his dogs into a kennel and took off on a murderous 8,000-mile journey.

• In Coral Gables, Florida, a twenty-three-year-old woman disappeared.

• In Melbourne, Florida, an aspiring model disappeared from a shopping center. Her body was later found, brutalized, in a swamp.

• In Tallahassee, Florida, a university student was abducted, raped, and tortured. She escaped from Wilder in Georgia.

It was the Tallahassee case that allowed a federal warrant to be issued against Wilder, and on April 5, 1984, the FBI named him to its Ten Most Wanted list.

But Wilder was not finished.

• In Beaumont, Texas, a woman was murdered, and her body was found in a ditch.
• In Oklahoma City, Oklahoma, a woman was abducted from a shopping center; her body was found in a lake.
• In Grand Junction, Colorado, a nineteen-year-old woman disappeared from a shopping center.
• In Las Vegas, Nevada, a seventeen-year-old girl was last seen alive with Wilder.
• In Torrance, California, a sixteen-year-old girl was abducted and abused on a cross-country trip; she was later released.
• In Merrilville, Indiana, a sixteen-year-old girl was abducted near a shopping mall. She was found in Penn Yan, New York, stabbed but alive.
• In Phelps, New York, a thirty-three-year-old woman was found slain on a rural road.

Finally, state police spotted Wilder at a gas station in New Hampshire. Wilder then drew a pistol from the glove compartment of his car and shot himself. When the bullet passed through his body and wounded one of the officers, he fired again and dropped dead.

Wilder's probation officer later said, "There were never any signs to pick up on. He was cleancut, cooperative, personable—never once lost his temper.

"With hindsight, this whole thing might look like it could have been prevented," the officer concluded. "But we get a lot of guys like Wilder. He was under care and doing well."

FBI

Christopher Wilder

Date: July 18, 1984

Site: San Ysidro, California

Type: Spree

Murderer: James Huberty

Victims: 21 people

....

Countless words were written about it, but few conveyed the scene as accurately as these from a five-year-old who lived through the worst one-day slaying by a lone gunman in United States history: "There was a war as McDonald's."

In the aftermath of that attack, the McDonald's restaurant in the San Diego neighborhood San Ysidro, California, on July 18, 1984, really did resemble a battlefield. For shortly after James Huberty opened fire on those inside and outside the busy restaurant, twenty-one people were dead and twenty more lay wounded on the floor.

Born in Ohio, in 1942, Huberty had lived an apparently normal life. He first studied embalming, and later worked in funeral homes, and then switched to welding. And along the way, he married and had two children.

When the welding plant he worked at closed in 1982, Huberty moved to Mexico, where he hoped to live cheaply. But he did not fit into the community. According to a friend, he was always talking about shooting someone, and he complained a lot about the Mexican policemen and others. Although he was able to get a job as a security guard licensed to carry firearms, he soon lost it.

Then, on July 18, after an outing with his family at the San Diego zoo, he put on camouflage pants and a shirt and told his wife, "I'm going to hunt humans." And off he went to McDonald's.

Huberty drove there in a truck that contained a small arsenal: a 12-gauge shotgun, a 9-mm semiautomatic Uzi submachine gun, and a 9-mm semiautomatic pistol. Fully armed, he burst into the restaurant, yelling, "Everybody get down on the floor or I'll kill somebody."

When the twenty-two-year-old store manager went to confront him, Huberty shot her dead with the shotgun. Then he began firing in earnest, spraying people in booths, shattering windows. Even after his victims fell to the ground, Huberty continued shooting at them. Unsuspecting children were hit as they walked their bikes to the entrance.

The first call to police came at 4:03 P.M., and the first car arrived at 4:07. Greeted with gunfire, the officer called for a full SWAT team. The police were reluctant to fire into the McDonald's, knowing there were innocent people still inside. The spiderweb effect of bullets on the shatterproof glass window of the storefront made visibility difficult. But the arrival of the police did at least draw the gunman's attention outside.

It was 5:05 P.M. before Huberty shot out an entire window panel, giving police the view they needed. At 5:17, atop a nearby building, a police sniper named Chuck Foster stood up and fired one shot from his .308-caliber sniper rifle, ripping into Huberty's aorta and killing him.

When the toll inside was finally taken, twenty people were dead and another nineteen wounded. Victims ranged in age from eighteen months to seventy-four years.

A great effort was spent not only to repair the wounded's physical damage, but to help them recover from their psychological trauma.

The restaurant site, meanwhile, was razed. A new McDonald's was built a quarter mile away.

Huberty's widow later asked for the return of the guns used in the incident, claiming she needed them for personal protection. The San Diego police refused.

Date: April 14, 1986

Site: Indianapolis, Indiana

Type: Spree

Murderer: Michael Wayne Jackson

Victims: Thomas Gahl, J.B. Hall, Earl Finn

....

PAROLE OFFICER Thomas Gahl was determined not to leave without the information he needed. He'd come to collect a urine sample to make sure that Michael Wayne Jackson was taking his medications and not using any illegal drugs. Gahl was pretty sure that Jackson was at home. So he kept knocking.

Jackson had been diagnosed as a schizophrenic. His police record of more than thirty arrests in seventeen years included convictions for such crimes as rape, sodomy, kidnapping, car theft, assault and battery, and shoplifting. He was known to have abused alcohol and been addicted to heroin.

Gahl was right: Jackson was home. One neighbor later reported hearing a scream and then a gunshot when Gahl came knocking on Jackson's door. Then someone was standing over a man in a suit who was lying on the ground and shouting, "Don't do it, don't do it!" Another shot rang out.

A second neighbor said he saw Gahl running away when the gunshot hit him and spun him around.

Jackson went back into his house, then reemerged, climbed into his truck, and left. At some point, he smeared his face with grease and spray-painted it and his hair. Then, only minutes after Jackson killed Gahl, the Indianapolis police received a report that he had struck again.

So began a spree that was to claim several more lives before it ended:

Jackson walked into a grocery store, put his shotgun to the grocer's head, and demanded money. The grocer gave him what he wanted, but Jackson killed him anyway.

Then he commandeered a car driven by a twenty-seven-year-old woman whom he held hostage for more than an hour, until she jumped from the moving car, breaking her leg but getting away in one piece.

Jackson was placed on the FBI's Most Wanted list on October 1, 1986. Radio reports and television programs gave his description, eliciting a tip from a viewer in O'Fallon, Missouri, forty miles north of St. Louis. The caller reported that a man who resembled Jackson had stolen several cars, assaulted some women in O'Fallon, and was headed toward Wright City.

When police in Wright City spotted one of the stolen cars, they gave chase. Jackson pointed a shotgun out the car window and fired. He hit a policeman with several pellets but did not hurt him seriously.

Another police officer continued the chase and finally found the car, abandoned, some time later. The driver of the car was also found—alive —locked in the trunk.

It was Jackson's raincoat that led police to him. The night he was captured, a police report said a man who resembled Jackson was seen hitchhiking wearing a blue raincoat. One of the policemen remembered seeing the coat hanging in an empty barn he'd searched earlier while looking for Jackson. When the police returned to the barn for another look, Jackson was there. Jackson couldn't be coaxed out of hiding, so they used tear gas to subdue and disorient him before storming the building. They found Jackson lying on the floor, his face nearly gone from a shotgun blast.

AP/Wide World Photos

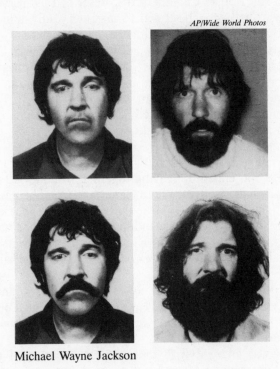

Michael Wayne Jackson

Date: August 26, 1986

Site: New York City

Type: Sex

Murderer: Robert Chambers, Jr.

Victim: Jennifer Levin

....

BOTH THE MURDERER and victim were young, well educated, and attractive. The crime was quickly dubbed The Preppie Murder. But there was nothing pretty about the partly clothed body found in New York City's Central Park on August 26, 1986.

The victim was identified as eighteen-year-old Jennifer Dawn Levin. Police were quickly directed to the man with whom she'd been seen leaving a bar in the early morning hours of August 26.

The man was Robert Chambers, Jr., described as a former Catholic altar boy, who had once belonged to an elite youth military marching group called the Knickerbocker Grays.

Despite his religious history and privileged background, Chambers had flunked out of several prestigious schools. A small-time thief, he was accused of rifling friends' jackets and teachers' purses. He was also treated twice for cocaine addiction.

Levin, meanwhile, had been voted "Best-Looking Girl" upon her graduation from a school in Baldwin, Long Island.

The two met and dated casually.

On the evening of August 26, Levin and Chambers bumped into each other at a bar and ended up leaving together around 4:30 A.M.

Levin's body was discovered hours later, and Chambers was eventually questioned. The police were particularly interested in the deep, fresh scratches on his face and chest, and his cut and bruised hands.

Chambers first told police that while he had indeed left the bar with Levin, he had parted from her quickly. The scratches, he said, were from his cat.

Under continued questioning, however, Chambers admitted having been with Levin in Central Park. He then claimed that Levin had "molested" him sexually, hurting his genitals, and that he had accidentally killed her during "rough sex."

Chambers was charged with murder, but the start of the trial was delayed by numerous motions from his high-powered defense lawyer. Opening statements were finally set for early January 1988.

The trial pitted a highly paid defense attorney against an experienced prosecutor known for her success in prosecuting rape cases. New York's complicated and stringent rules of evidence prevented the use of what might have been incriminating facts about Chambers—his past alcoholism and cocaine addiction, for example. After all the testimony had been heard, the trial jury became deadlocked for nine days. At that point, the prosecution and defense agreed on a plea-bargaining arrangement, in which Chambers pleaded guilty to manslaughter.

According to the prosecution, Jennifer Levin's parents had agreed to the bargaining in an effort to avoid a mistrial and any further strain on the family.

When the judge asked Chambers, twenty-one at the time, if he had intended to cause "serious injury" to Levin, he replied, "Looking back on everything, I have to say yes. It breaks my heart to have to say that."

Adding to the already sensational nature of the case, which was publicized throughout the nation, was a videotape of a New Year's Day party in which Chambers was seen cavorting with four young women in pajamas, underwear, and lingerie. The group mugged for the camera, and in one segment, Chambers was seen playing with a small doll. Leering at the camera, he twisted off the doll's head and said, "I think I've killed it."

Chambers was sentenced to five to fifteen years in prison.

FBI

Robert Chambers, Jr.

Date: November 1, 1987

Site: Greenwich Village, New York City

Type: Child Abuse

Murderer: Joel Steinberg

Victim: Lisa Steinberg

··

THE VICTIM WAS a defenseless six-year-old girl and the murderer was a well-educated lawyer, who by some accounts was a millionaire. He was also her adoptive father.

Not only had Joel Steinberg beaten the child, but he'd also victimized his companion, Hedda Nussbaum, and mistreated his adopted son Michael.

When paramedics found little Lisa Steinberg lying on the bathroom floor in a Greenwich Village apartment, accounts of the violence spread throughout the country. Lisa died several days later.

Joel Steinberg, in his mid-forties, had been a successful lawyer until he was disbarred. In that capacity, he had helped arrange the adoption of a newborn child in 1981. The unmarried mother, who was Catholic and had rejected the option of abortion, gave the child to Steinberg after he promised to place it with a good Catholic family.

Instead, Steinberg took the baby to his own apartment, which he shared with Hedda Nussbaum, a children's book editor. Steinberg never formally adopted the child he called Lisa. Certainly no adoption agency would have approved the adoptive home: Both Steinberg and Nussbaum were cocaine addicts. The apartment was filthy. Steinberg regularly beat Nussbaum, whose bruises were glaringly visible at his trial.

Steinberg apparently beat young Lisa, too. Neighbors had long been worried about the family, and one of Lisa's teachers had contacted the New York City Bureau of Child Welfare on her behalf. Yet no action was taken against Steinberg. On November 1, 1987, Steinberg hit Lisa until she was comatose because, according to Nussbaum, she kept staring at him. He then left her lying on the bathroom floor.

Instructing Nussbaum not to touch the child until he got back, Steinberg left the house. Hours later he returned and used cocaine with Nussbaum before finally, at about 6:30 A.M., allowing her to call for help.

The child died three days later.

Steinberg and Nussbaum were both arrested, but only Steinberg was prosecuted. During the trial, people who knew them described Nussbaum as Steinberg's victim and their eleven-year relationship as rapidly deteriorating. According to several witnesses—Nussbaum herself among them—Steinberg had brainwashed her, deprived her of food, and meted out other more bizarre punishments for imagined transgressions.

But because Nussbaum had not actually seen Steinberg strike Lisa, he was found guilty only of manslaughter.

At his sentencing, Steinberg gave a rambling monologue in his own defense. The judge, however, cut him off and handed him the maximum sentence, from eight and a third to twenty-five years in prison, recommending that Steinberg not be paroled until he'd served all twenty-five years.

AP/Wide World Photos

Joel Steinberg

Date: April 17, 1989

Site: Kirtland, Ohio

Type: Cult

Murderers: Jeffrey, Alice, and Damon Lundgren

Victims: Dennis, Cheryl, Rebecca, Trina, and Karen Avery

....

WHEN JEFFREY LUNDGREN was convicted of the five murders, he asserted that it was God who had ordered him to kill Dennis and Cheryl Avery and their three young daughters.

"It's not a figment of my imagination that I can in fact talk to God, that I can hear His voice," the forty-year-old Lundgren said. "In fact, all the prophets were commanded to specific acts."

In the late 1980s, Lundgren had moved from Independence, Missouri to Kirtland, Ohio, where he and other dissident members of the Mormon Church joined the Reorganized Church. Lundgren became a lay minster in the Reorganized Church, but his status had been revoked for teaching radical doctrines. Lundgren left that church too, to found a cult of his own.

The Averys and their children were bound, gagged, shot one at a time, and then buried in a common grave in a barn. A church official in Ohio said he thought the slayings resulted from a dispute over money, sex, or fear that the Averys were about to leave the cult. But during her own trial Alice Lundgren testified that her husband had spoken of killing the Averys as a sacrifice that would make it possible for cult members to see God.

The Lundgrens were arrested in January 1990, near the Mexican border. Authorities found an assault rifle, ammunition, knives, and gas masks in their motel room and in a storage locker. The Lundgrens were also well-stocked with camping gear—"things that can sustain you in the mountains," according to one official.

Jeffrey Lundgren was sentenced to death after being convicted on five counts of aggravated murder; his wife, Alice, was sentenced to five consecutive life terms, and his son, Damon, who was nineteen at the time of the murders, was sentenced to four consecutive life terms.

Date: August 23, 1989
Site: Brooklyn, New York
Type: Racial
Murderer: Joseph Fama
Victim: Yusef Hawkins

••

VIOLENCE OF WHITE against black is an old story in the United States, but it is a story that nearly everyone had hoped was a part of the past. Unfortunately, in the case of Yusef Hawkins, the past seemed very much a part of the present.

On August 23, 1989, according to police reports, Hawkins, a sixteen-year-old black American, and three black friends came to the Bensonhurst neighborhood of Brooklyn, New York, to look at a used car that was for sale.

A mob of ten to thirty white youths from the mostly white neighborhood surrounded the four blacks, shouting racial epithets and chasing them with baseball bats. One member of the group pulled out a gun and fired four shots, hitting Hawkins twice and killing him.

Keith Mondello, the white group's ringleader, said that he had had an argument with a former girlfriend who had been dating Hispanics and blacks, he had been told that a group of her Hispanic and black friends were coming to beat him up.

Mondello said he then rounded up thirty friends at "Sal the Squid's," a streetfront candy store in his girlfriend's apartment building, warning them that a bunch of her friends were coming to beat him up. Unfortunately, it was Hawkins and his friends who unknowingly walked into this atmosphere.

The murder immediately became a national event, with newspaper columnists and TV reporters throughout the country commenting on it and an angry public demanding rapid justice.

It took more than a year and a half of legal proceedings, however, to prosecute eight people on various charges, and only one of them was convicted of murder. Joseph Fama, nineteen, was found guilty of second-degree murder. He was sentenced to twenty-five years in prison. Other boys in the white group were found guilty of lesser charges, including Mondello. Three others were acquitted.

It took the jury ten days of deliberation to convict Mondello on eleven counts, including riot, weapons possession, and discrimination—but excluding murder.

When the verdict was announced, Hawkins's mother, Diane Hawkins, moaned and fell forward. Some of the family's supporters jumped up and swore loudly. Outside the courthouse, another group set an American flag afire to chants of "Burn Bensonhurst, burn!" and some later went on a rampage, smashing windows and trashing a Korean grocery.

Date: September 1, 1989
Site: Gainesville, Florida
Type: Revenge
Murderer: Jens Peter Hansen
Victim: Arthur Kimura

....

JENS PETER HANSEN was denied a doctorate in pathology in 1989.

A little more than a year later, Hansen struck back at the professor who was the chairman of the academic committee at the University of Florida at Gainesville that refused him a degree, Arthur Kimura, a cancer researcher.

Kimura and other members of the committee had voted to drop Hansen from the Ph.D. program because he was straying from his goal and conducting low-quality research.

Hansen armed himself with a rope, a pistol, and a baseball bat and drove to Kimura's house. He planned to knock the professor out and then to make it look like he'd committed suicide. He would put the unconscious Kimura in his car in his garage with the engine running.

But things did not go according to plan: Kimura apparently tripped a burglar alarm when Hansen appeared, and Hansen responded by shooting him in the head, killing him. The burglar alarm brought the police, and Hansen was arrested only minutes later.

His attorney argued that he was insane when he devised his plan to murder Kimura, but the state prosecutor disagreed. "What caused the tragedy was a monumental ego and a revengeful spirit," the prosecutor said.

The jury agreed. Hansen, forty-two at the time of the trial, was found guilty of first-degree murder and sentenced to a minimum of twenty-five years in prison.

Date: October 23, 1989

Site: Boston, Massachusetts

Type: Fraud

Murderer: Charles Stuart

Victim: Carol Stuart

....

THE DRAMATIC STORY of how a wounded Boston man, Charles Stuart, valiantly fought to save his dying, pregnant wife after they were violently attacked by a robber—-calling the police on a cellular car phone and talking until he faded into unconsciousness, and how the police finally found the pair by listening to sirens they heard on the phone, made headlines throughout the United States.

The excitement was dimmed only hours later, however, by the death of Carol Stuart, whose baby was delivered prematurely by Caesarean section after she'd been brought to the hospital with a severe head wound. The baby, too, would eventually die.

Stuart had described the attacker as a black man, and in the hours following the slaying, Boston police were accused of going from door to door in the Mission Hill section where the incident occurred and indiscriminately harassing black men.

The case appeared to be closed when Stuart, a twenty-nine-year-old furrier who had received a stomach wound in the incident finally picked a black man out of a police lineup. Only months later, however, the entire nation found itself the victim of a colossal hoax that brought accusations of murder along with cries of racism. For in early January, Charles Stuart's brother, Matthew, went to the police with information implicating Charles Stuart himself in the murder of his wife.

The sensational turned bizarre the next day, when Charles Stuart apparently parked his car on the Tobin Bridge in Boston during morning rush-hour traffic and jumped to his death.

Matthew Stuart, twenty-three, then revealed that his brother had given him a bag containing a revolver and some of Carol Stuart's personal belongings, including an engagement ring that Charles had reported stolen during the "robbery."

In the days following Stuart's suicide, authorities concluded that money had been at the core of the killing. They said that Charles Stuart had collected $83,000 from an insurance policy on his wife's life and there were said to be more policies still outstanding.

Blacks in Boston reacted angrily to the news, accusing the police of being much too quick to pursue the stereotypical suspect in a city racked by racism. The man chosen from the police lineup and charged with the murder was of course cleared by Stuart's suicide. But that wasn't the end of it as far as he was concerned.

"My life and may family's lives have been ruined, and no one is willing to take responsibility," the falsely accused man said. And community leaders from the Mission Hills neighborhood called for an apology. "We want it to go nationwide," a spokesperson said.

And then, late in 1991, after months of investigation, Matthew Stuart was indicted and charged with conspiracy to obstruct justice and with compounding a felony.

Date: December 16 and 18, 1989

Site: Mountain Brook, Alabama; Savannah, Georgia

Type: Assassination

Murderer: Walter Leroy Moody, Jr.

Victims: U.S. Circuit Court Judge Robert Vance;
Robert E. Robinson

....

LESS THAN A WEEK before Christmas in 1989, U.S. Circuit Court Judge Robert Vance died when a package mailed to his home in Mountain Brook, Alabama, exploded. Two days later, another mailed bomb killed Robert E. Robinson, a civil rights lawyer and city alderman in Savannah, Georgia.

Before the bombings, a group calling itself Americans for a Competent Federal Judicial System wrote to the major news organizations, threatening to kill lawyers, judges, and officials of the National Association for the Advancement of Colored People. Investigators said the letters bore similar markings and were sent from several locations in Georgia.

In later letters, the group claimed it had assassinated the judge and attorney in reprisal for "atrocities" committed against a white woman who was robbed, raped, and murdered in Atlanta in 1988.

The letters also expressed anger over a school desegregation case in DeKalb County, Georgia, that Judge Vance had presided over. The appellate panel had ordered the school system to transfer white teachers to schools with predominantly black student populations.

Two other bombs, one sent to the NAACP in Jacksonville, Florida, and the other to officers of the 11th Circuit Court in Atlanta, were defused.

In November 1990, the Justice Department announced a seventy-count indictment against Walter Leroy Moody, Jr., of Rex, Georgia, charging that Moody had hatched the plot in revenge against the judicial system for convicting him for unlawfully possessing a pipe bomb.

In 1972, Moody and his wife, Susan, were accused of conspiracy and obstruction of justice in a scheme to induce a federal court in Macon, Georgia, to vacate Moody's 1972 conviction. Moody had been charged after the pipe bomb went off in his home, injuring his then-wife, Hazel. He served two years in federal prison.

When Moody went to trial in June 1991 for the mail-bomb murders, the prosecution accused him of waging a "full-fledged, publicly announced war" against the legal system. Believing that blacks received preferential treatment in the courts, Moody had targeted his victims because they'd been involved in civil rights cases.

Moody was the only defense witness, taking the stand against the advice of his court-appointed lawyers. He blamed the Ku Klux Klan for the bombings and said he had been unwittingly used by his former attorney to get parts for the bombs.

A jury convicted him of all seventy-one counts, including murder. One juror described Moody as "scary" and "calculated." Many others felt his testimony had been riddled with lies.

Moody was sentenced to seven consecutive life terms plus four hundred years in prison.

Date: May 16, 1990

Site: Santa Monica, California

Type: Celebrity

Murderer: Christian Brando

Victim: Dag Drollet

....

CHRISTIAN BRANDO never made it as a movie star, but in one real-life drama his name did play above that of his famous father, actor Marlon Brando. Unfortunately, the headlines emblazoned across the country made Christian infamous rather than famous. He was arrested for the murder of his half-sister's boyfriend.

According to police reports, the young Brando admitted firing the .45-caliber gun that killed Dag Drollet, a twenty-six-year-old guest at the home of actor Marlon Brando, where the incident took place.

The elder Brando, his wife, Tarita Taripia, and his daughter, Cheyenne, were home at the time and heard the gunshot. No one, however, witnessed the shooting.

Christian and his half-sister Cheyenne, who was pregnant at the time, had apparently dined together a few hours before the shooting, at which time Cheyenne reportedly complained about Drollet abusing her.

Marlon Brando tried to revive Drollet with mouth-to-mouth resuscitation before calling the police about five minutes after the shooting. When police arrived, they found Drollet's body in what was described as the entertainment room. They also found an apparently calm Christian Brando, the murder weapon, and several other firearms—including an M-14 carbine, a shotgun, and an Uzi assault rifle—all reportedly belonging to Christian, who was a gun enthusiast.

Christian Brando appeared in court unshaven and dressed in a shirt and jeans. He pleaded not guilty to a charge of first-degree murder.

One month later, Cheyenne flew to a Polynesian island the day after prosecutors in Los Angeles attempted to serve her with court papers naming her as a material witness in the case. Before leaving the country, she had reportedly told police the killing was not accidental.

Prosecutors also admitted that the police had bungled the investigation by failing to advise the defendant of his rights before he made a lengthy statement—a statement therefore inadmissible in court.

It was determined that the trial could be held without Cheyenne, who was beyond the reach of U.S. law. In any case, by early in November

1990, she was comatose in a Tahitian hospital having overdosed on tranquilizers and antidepressant drugs.

On January 4, 1992, Christian Brando agree to plead guilty to a charge
of voluntary manslaughter. The district attorney accepted the plea after
failing to convince Cheyenne's lawyers to deliver their witness. The lawyers claimed that due to her physical and mental condition she would not
be available as a witness in the foreseeable future.

Cheyenne, who gave birth to Drollet's child in Tahiti, was rumored to
have twice attempted suicide after her boyfriend's death.

Brando is awaiting sentencing.

Date: August 15 and 26, 1990; June 6, 1991

Site: Gainesville, Florida

Type: Serial

Murderer: Unknown

Victims: Christina Powell, Sonja Larson, Christa Hoyt, Tracy Paules, and Manuel Taboada; Eleanor Grace and Carla McKishnie

....

LAW ENFORCEMENT TECHNIQUES have advanced quickly, so when five students were brutally murdered within twenty-four hours in Gainesville, Florida, an army of investigators including the FBI expert who worked on the Ted Bundy (see page 115) and Son of Sam (see page 125) cases, descended on the college town.

But despite some early progress in naming a suspect, one year and two murders later, no one has been charged with the crimes.

The police called the killer a "methodical maniac" who slipped inside windows and doors, attacking slim brunettes in three separate attacks.

The first victims were Christina Powell, seventeen, and Sonja Larson, eighteen, both students at the University of Florida, plus Christa Hoyt, eighteen, a Santa Fe Community College student. All were slain within hours of each other. The next day, two more students were killed: Tracy Paules, twenty-three, of the University of Florida, and Manuel Taboada, twenty-three, of Santa Fe Community College.

Three of the five bodies were mutilated, and the killer had apparently left a message. According to authorities, "He was very calculated, very methodical in a the way the person did things, as well as left things." They did not elaborate further.

The murders caused a panic in the college community. Some students dropped out of school, and others bought weapons and went to great lengths to secure their apartments and rooms.

In June 1991, two more female students were killed, Eleanor Grace and Carla McKishnie, and once again fear pervaded the college campus. But police denied that there was a connection between the two cases.

A twenty-nine year old carpet cleaner was charged with the murders of Grace and McKishnie, but not with the earlier murders. Authorities said that the suspect had gone to the students' apartment to clean rugs and strangled the women after they sprayed him with Mace. They did not say why the women had attacked the suspect.

Just a week before the June 1991 murders, another person (in jail for beating his grandmother) had been named as the prime suspect in the five previous murders. As it turned out, the two suspects had links to each other; both had been imprisoned in Florida at the same time for other crimes.

Still, neither suspect was charged with the murders of the first five victims.

Date: November 5, 1990

Site: New York, New York

Type: Assassination

Murderer: El Sayyid Nosair

Victim: Rabbi Meir Kahane

··

As FOUNDER OF the militant Jewish Defense League, Rabbi Meir Kahane was one of the best known and most controversial of Jewish militants. His message "Never Again" became a battled cry for Jewish activism, reminding the world of the Holocaust.

That same message, however, drew him the enmity of many. On November 5, 1990, after addressing a Zionist group, Kahane was shot in the neck with a .357 Magnum by a lone gunman in the Marriott East Side Hotel in New York City.

After he'd also shot a seventy-three-year-old bystander in the leg, the gunman jumped into a taxi and rode a block before getting out and opening fire on a postal service worker. The postal worker returned the fire, hitting the gunman in the chin.

The wounded gunman, thirty-four-year-old El Sayyid Nosair, was then arrested. Police said he had acted alone in the murder and had no links to any Mideast terrorist organization. Nosair lived in Cliffside Park, New Jersey, and repaired heating and air-conditioning equipment for New York City.

Kahane's funeral, in Jerusalem, set off a riot when hundreds of his supporters broke away from the procession and rampaged through the city, shouting "Death to Arabs." The rioters stabbed and beat Arabs, smashed shop windows, and clashed with police. At one point, they tried to hold back an ambulance that was attempting to rescue a fallen Arab.

In November 1990, Nosair was charged with second-degree murder, attempted murder, assaulting a police officer, second-degree assault, criminal possession of a weapon, reckless endangerment, and coercion.

According to his family, he had been depressed because even though he had an engineering degree, he was hired to do what he considered menial labor.

During a court appearance in May 1991, the slain Kahane's son, Binyamin, and four other men charged to the front of the courtroom in an attempt to get at Nosair. Court officers pushed Nosair to the floor and he escaped injury, but a spectator was hurt in the scuffle. Though Binyamin was not arrested, the four Kahane supporters were.

Later, speaking to reporters, Binyamin Kahane said of Nosair: "He has to be killed. According to Jewish law, this is what he deserves."

Nosair was acquitted of Kahane's murder by a jury in New York City, but he was found guilty of wounding two people as he fled the scene. He received a prison term of up to twenty-two years.

Date: April 15, 1991

Site: Bellevue, Washington

Type: Revenge

Murderer: Beryl Challis

Victim: Dr. Selwyn Cohen

....

A SIXTY-YEAR-OLD suburban housewife named Beryl Challis had an appointment with the plastic surgeon who had performed her face lift, Dr. Selwyn Cohen. She left after thirty minutes—the visit was routine.

Later, Challis came back. The staff had left for the day, but Dr. Cohen was still there, and Challis persuaded him to let her in. When he did, she killed him—shooting him five times with a .38-caliber pistol she'd bought three weeks before.

Then she left the office and went home. She told her husband, Albert, sixty-four, that she wanted to go out and get something to eat, and she left again. Not long afterward, Albert discovered a note she had left in their bedroom. It said, "I have a wonderful husband and two lovely sons and everything to live for, but you have ruined my face and hair and mutilated my face muscles and put me in this constant pain. I feel that life is not worth living this way, and I will take my life. But it is you, Dr. Cohen, with your dreadful radical surgery, that have killed me."

Frantic, Albert drove to a nearby restaurant to look for his wife, but she wasn't there, so he returned home to wait for her. When he arrived she was already there, dying of a self-inflicted gunshot wound to the head.

Dr. Cohen had operated on Challis in 1990. (She had chosen him after seeing him on television.) Her face lift was described as an ordinary procedure, one the doctor, who was forty-one years old at the time of his death, had performed many times.

Most patients experience only minor transitory discomfort after a face lift, but Challis's experience was different. Her face felt as if she were wearing an iron mask. She described the pain as searing; changes of temperature made her feel as though she were being cut. She thought her skin was very dry and that veins had started to appear on the surface.

Cohen referred Challis to three other surgeons and to a counselor. One of the doctors, Gilman Middleton, said that he could find no physical cause for her pain, and that how she looked was "a matter of opinion." He acknowledged, however, that she was suffering.

Members of Cohen's office staff said that Challis "had a good result" in terms of appearance, but that she could not be convinced of that. And her husband said she was "a very vain woman" who expected her face lift to be a "minor tune-up." Instead, she had become so ashamed of the way she looked that she became a recluse who took to her bed wishing for death.

Date: October 17, 1991

Site: Killeen, Texas

Type: Mass

Murderer: George Hennard

Victims: 22 People

....

A NINETEEN-YEAR-OLD employee emerged safely from a hiding spot in a commercial dishwasher twenty hours after the worst mass slaying in the history of the United States drove patrons and employees out windows and into corners.

The employee's first words when he climbed out of the dishwasher were, "Did the Braves win?" referring to the baseball playoffs.

The employee had sought his hiding spot after a gunman drove his pickup truck into the front window of Luby's Cafeteria in Killeen, Texas, a town of 45,000 in the heart of the state.

The gunman, George Hennard, got out of his truck and began firing a seventeen-shot 9 mm Glock semi-automatic pistol at cafeteria employees and patrons. Responding to reports of the shooting, the police arrived and exchanged fire with Hennard and wounded him. Then Hennard put his gun to his own head and fired, killing himself. When it was over—after ten minutes—he had shot and killed twenty-two other people and wounded at least twenty more.

Hennard, thirty-five, who came from nearby Belton, Texas, revealed no clear motive for the murders at the scene, although he was heard to say "This is what Bell County did to me." Nor were the reasons found in his home after the spree or in interviews with his family and neighbors. His mother said she had talked to him only a few days before the killings, on his thirty-fifth birthday, and that he had seemed fine. A psychiatrist who had treated him in 1989 said "I was really as shocked as anybody else. No way in the world to anticipate that it would come to this."

Hennard was known as a loner who terrorized neighbors with bizarre, but hitherto harmless, behavior. He had no criminal record. It was clear that he strongly disliked women.

Fourteen of the twenty-two killed were women, and one witness to the murders said that Hennard had stepped past men to shoot women, many of them at point-blank range, and in the head.